HOW TO RAISE AND TRAIN A SHIH TZU

H.M. Queen Elizabeth (now the Queen Mother) holds Choo-Choo as the family poses (1936) on the lawn of Royal Lodge Windsor. Photo by Lisa Sheridan.

By R. H. Smythe, M.R.C.V.S.

Distributed in the U.S.A. by T.F.H. Publications, Inc., 211 West Sylvania Avenue, P.O. Box 27, Neptune City, N.J. 07753; in England by T.F.H. (Gt. Britain) Ltd., 13 Nutley Lane, Reigate, Surrey; in Canada to the book store and library trade by Clarke, Irwin & Company, Clarwin House, 791 St. Clair Avenue West, Toronto 10, Ontario; in Canada to the pet trade by Rolf C. Hagen Ltd., 3225 Sartelon Street, Montreal 382, Quebec; in Southeast Asia by Y.W. Ong, 9 Lorong 36 Geylang, Singapore 14; in Australia and the south Pacific by Pet Imports Pty. Ltd., P.O. Box 149, Brookvale 2100, N.S.W., Australia. Published by T.F.H. Publications. Inc. Ltd.; The British Crown Colony of Hong Kong.

ACKNOWLEDGEMENTS

It gives me great pleasure to express thanks to . . .

Her Majesty Queen Elizabeth, the Queen Mother, who, as one of the first to introduce the Shih Tzu to the western world, has very kindly expressed her interest in this book and has supplied photographs . . .

Lady Haggerston, who has been very helpful . . .

Mrs. Audrey Fowler, who has supplied much information and a number of photos . . .

Bill and Joan Kibler, for their invaluable information on the history of the Shih Tzu . . .

Mr. and Mrs. Bill Jobson, who have been towers of strength in providing a considerable portion of the manuscript and in collecting photographs for illustrations.

I have been very cheered by the vast amount of cooperation I have received from everyone (far too many to mention here) connected with the breed, but to each of them I express my sincere thanks.

ISBN 0-87666-388-9

CONTENTS

The Shih Tzu when properly groomed somewhat resembles a miniature lion. Photo by Louise Van der Meid.

1. History and Standard

"LION DOGS"

The name Shih Tzu (pronounced "sheed zoo"), given to the breed by the Chinese, means Tibetan Lion Dog. It must not be imagined that the Chinese were greatly perturbed by the presence of lions or that they bred these little dogs for the purpose of slaying lions. The most widely accepted theory as to the origin of the name "Lion Dog" is that the breed, when suitably combed and trimmed, could be made up into a creditable representation of a miniature lion.

There are several breeds of short-faced long-haired Asiatic "Lion Dogs" whose lineages go back several or many centuries. These include such breeds as the Shih Tzu, Lhasa Apso, and Pekingese (and, possibly, the Japanese Spaniel). Another breed with similar body conformation, but lacking the long hair, is the Pug.

Lion Dogs, unlike so many other breeds in China, were protected throughout their lives, accorded very high honor, and guarded by eunuchs, and even by the army. They were kept in the best part of the Imperial Palace, they slept upon the richest silk, and they fed from the Emperor's personal table.

ORIGIN OF THE SHIH TZU

During the Manchu Dynasty (founded in 1583) it was the custom of the Dalai Lama of Tibet to send propitiatory presents of highly-prized Apsos to the powerful Emperor of China. In addition, Manchu generals who returned from successful invasions of Tibet during the eighteenth century made a practice of bringing these dogs back as spoils of war. Such dogs were placed, with great ceremony, at the feet of the Emperor as symbols of Manchu victories by junior officers who had played the more successful roles in the campaign. The foundation stock of the Shih Tzu was probably these Tibetan Apsos of the Chinese royal palace and the native Chinese Pekingese.

Crossbreeding, however, may have been more extensive than has been generally imagined, and whether or not this was intentional is uncertain. In the Imperial Palace of Pekin there were other short-faced dogs in addition to the Imperial Pekingese. One of these was the smooth-coated breed that was the forerunner of our modern Pug. The Pug is reputed to have been used to breed the original bull-fighting Bulldog down to the squat, scowling gentleman we know today. Unlikely as it may seem that there should be any relationship between the Shih Tzu and the Bulldog, this becomes far less extraordinary when one compares the body of the Shih Tzu beneath its heavy coating of hair with that of the modern Bulldog. One has only in the mind's eye to diminish the size of the Bulldog and provide it with a heavy coat to recognize a likeness between the two breeds.

CHINESE GROOMING METHODS

The Shih Tzu's coat came mainly from the Tibetan Apsos and partly from the Pekingese; the lion-like shape was probably accentuated by crosses with the short-haired Puglike form.

It is recorded that the Chinese not only gave the newly produced breed the title of "Shih Tzu" but also made further efforts to make the resemblance more realistic by means of the "lion clip." To accomplish this they left all the hair on the head and shoulders, but clipped the hair on the rest of the body close.

In the Chinese Imperial Palace at Pekin, the care of these dogs was in the hands of eunuchs who devoted a great deal of time grooming and tending their charges. It was their custom, apparently, to comb out the dog's beards and moustaches away from the face and rough up the hair behind the head and on the shoulders to form a lion-like mane. The "chrysanthemum" growth of hair from the upper surface of the nose would then be plaited into the hair that descended from the forehead. The result was that the face became completely hidden beneath a mop of hair that covered the eyes and made it almost impossible for the dog to see anything at all unless peepholes were provided in front of the eyes.

When the grooming had been successfully done, the court artists were engaged to produce illuminated scrolls depicting the most outstanding examples not only of the breed but also of the art of the court hairdresser. It was considered a very great honor when the picture of some particularly remarkable specimen was recorded in the Imperial Dog Book. A number of illuminated scrolls depicting the success of the eunuchs in producing such dogs and dressing their coats in the fashion of the times are still to be found in the hands of collectors.

THE ARRIVAL OF THE SHIH TZU IN BRITAIN AND AMERICA

It was not until 1930 that the first pair of Shih Tzus was imported into England by General Sir Douglas and Lady Brownrigg. These were a dog, Hibou, and a bitch, Shu-Ssa. It was also in 1930 that Miss Hutchins imported into Ireland Lung-Fu-Ssu, a male. In 1934 the Shih Tzu Club was founded, with the Countess of Essex as its President and Lady Brownrigg as Secretary. The first Championships were awarded in 1940. Some dissatisfaction was expressed about this time about the size of the dogs, and in 1956 the Manchu Shih Tzu Club was formed, a private society desirous of looking after the interests of the smaller type more in keeping with those originally bred in the palace at Pekin. In 1958 the Shih Tzu Club of England agreed to permit its standard to include these smaller specimens.

There is no record of any Shih Tzus reaching the United States much before 1950, although some claim that introductions were made about the

English Ch. Ellingham Kala Hag went Best of Breed at the 1963 Crufts show in England. The champion was bred and is owned by Lady Haggerston. Photo by C. M. Cooke and Son.

time that they first arrived in England. If so, the records are no longer available. A considerable number reached the United States from 1950 onward, not only from England but also from France, Sweden, and Denmark. In 1955 the American Kennel Club recognized the Shih Tzu as a distinct breed and allowed them to be shown in the Miscellaneous Class. In 1957 the Shih Tzu Club of America came into being. Other clubs have begun to spring up, notably the Texas Tzu Society, founded in 1960. The American Kennel Club agreed that until such time as the A.K.C. permits registry of the Shih Tzu, the English standard of show points should be adopted. Between 1930 and 1960, more than 1,300 Shih Tzus were registered in England. There were about 300 Shih Tzus in the United States at the end of 1963.

Some of the later importations into Britain following the earliest already mentioned included Tashi of Chouette, a bitch imported by the Earl of Essex in 1938, and Choo-Choo, a dog presented by the Danish Ministry to H.M. Queen Elizabeth, the Queen Mother, in 1933, while she was the Duchess of York. Other importations were three bitches, all imported by Gen. Telfer-Smollet: Ming, in 1939; Ishuh Tzu, in 1948; and Hsing Erh, in 1952. Mr. R. P. Dobson brought over Hsi-Li-Ya in 1952, and Mrs. M. Longden introduced Jungfaltets Yung-Ming from Sweden in 1959.

The reason the Shih Tzu was not heard of earlier is that it was almost impossible to obtain one during the reigns of the Chinese emperors; the dogs were the personal property of the royal family, and anyone attempting to acquire one by unlawful means was promptly put to death.

The Lhasa Apso, very similar or possibly identical to the progenitor of the Shih Tzu, reached Britain through India from Tibet.

SIMILARITY TO THE LHASA APSO

The Shih Tzu and the Lhasa Apso are similar in size, standing from 9-11 inches in height. The Shih Tzu has a broad round skull with considerable width between the eyes, and not more than an inch of foreface; the Apso has a narrow skull and a fairly long foreface, 1½ inches in length measured from nose tip to lower corner of the eye. The Shih Tzu has a well-defined stop, but in the Apso this is absent and the skull falls away behind the eye. The eye of the Apso is smaller and not sunk in, terrier fashion. The ears of the Apso originate high on the skull; those of the Shih Tzu are set low and drooping. The Apso coat is more harsh and the tail is carried over the back in a screw; in the Shih Tzu the tail itself is fairly short, but carries a great amount of hair, giving the appearance of great length. The Apso is higher in the leg, much finer in bone, and longer in the back. The muzzle of the Shih Tzu is square and deep; in the Apso it is longer and must not be square.

1952 PEKINGESE CROSS

The first intentional crossbreeding (or is it really backcrossing?) of a Shih Tzu with a Pekingese took place in Britain, in 1952. It was felt that the Shih Tzu breed was deteriorating and that the introduction of fresh blood was imperative.

Lady Haggerston of Chathill, Northumberland, has stated that the crossing was necessary because there were very few Shih Tzus in Britain and the breed was in danger of becoming seriously inbred. Shih Tzus of that time had poor bone structure and pigmentation, and they also suffered from "pinched nostrils"—a bad fault in the Shih Tzu. The cross had the desired effect and improved the breed to such an extent that it gave rise to an almost immediate desire by the public to possess these fascinating little creatures. They do not resemble the Pekingese in any way whatsoever in character or coat.

Joan and Bill Kibler point out in their brochure on the history of the Shih Tzu that old Chinese prints display short-legged dogs with the head heavily bearded and moustached, quite unlike the smooth forehead of the Pekingese. There is no evidence that the modern Shih Tzu, carrying recent Pekingese blood, is in any danger of losing the characteristic "chrysanthemum" appearance created by the crop of hair that grows upward from the foreface between eye and nose. Nor has any loss of hair on the forehead itself occurred, causing the dog to resemble a Pekingese in appearance.

The fourth generation removed from the Pekingese cross is considered by the English Kennel Club as being pure Shih Tzu, but it was only in 1957 that this rule was introduced, and certain Pekingese characteristics may well appear in the breed up to the fifth, sixth, or even later generations.

Foundation Lines of the Shih Tzu

Mrs. L. G. Widdrington, a prominent English breeder, has extensive records of the breed, and according to her records all our present-day Shih Tzus descend from ten dogs; about ten other dogs have also been imported, but their lines have not been continued.

The following are the lines and dogs from which the present stock descends: (d. = dog; b. = bitch).

HIBOU, d.	1930	Imported from China by Lt.-General Sir Douglas and Lady Brownrigg.
SHU-SSA, b.	1930	Ditto.
LUNG-FU-SSU, d.	1930	Imported from China by Miss Hutchins (Ireland).
		(All Shih Tzus contain these three lines).
CHOO-CHOO, d.	1933	Presented to H.M. Queen Elizabeth, the Queen Mother, by the Danish Ministry in Norway.
TASHI CHOUETTE, b.	1938	Imported from China by the Rt. Hon. The Earl of Essex.
MING, b.	1939	Imported from China by Lt.-General Telfar-Smollett, Lord Lieu of Dunbartonshire.
ISHUH TZU, b.	1948	Ditto.
PHILADELPHUS SUTI-T'SUN of ELFANN, d. (A Pekingese)		
	1952	The Pekingese cross introduced to the breed by Miss E. M. Evans.
HSI-LI-YA, b.	1952	Imported from China by Mr. R. P. Dobson.
JUNGFALTETS JUNG-MING, d.	1952	Imported from Sweden by Mrs. M. Longden.

Of these ten dogs from which our stock descends, five were imported with "pedigree unknown" and three more with their pedigrees recorded for only one generation.

In accordance with the rules of the English Kennel Club, an import with "pedigree unknown" may be registered on the recommendation of a specialist judge that it is a typical specimen of its breed. Mated with a partner recognized also as "purebred," the offspring of such a union can obtain class registration.

Three of the Shih Tzus carrying Pekingese "blood" in present-day English pedigrees are: TEE-NI TIM OF MICHELCOMBE, d.; SHIH WEI TZU OF ELFANN, b.; and MU-HO, b.

It is interesting to note that all three of the third crossbred generation named above have been bred from considerably, and therefore many Shih Tzus contain this line.

In England all subsequent generations after the third crossbred generation get a Class One registration with the English Kennel Club and are termed "purebred" Shih Tzus.

The American Kennel Club has no such liberal philosophy. They will not recognize any import of this breed without a *ten-generation* purebred Shih Tzu pedigree. This is a most restrictive ordinance as regards the British breeder.

It would appear that a lot of unnecessary fuss has been made about the Pekingese cross, if we compare what has taken place in the Shih Tzu with what has happened without comment in so many other breeds.

We wonder why there should be any occasion to quibble about the introduction of a little more Pekingese blood into a breed that already contains it. It might be worth one's life to attend a show in Britain as a spectator and make the innocent remark that the Shih Tzus resembled Pekingese.

The Pekingese may introduce a face wrinkle, which must be avoided according to the modern standard, and it may bring in bowed front legs, but the standard says nothing as to whether the forelegs shall be straight or bandy so long as they are short and muscular with ample bone and "look massive" on account of the wealth of hair.

It appears unlikely that the Pekingese cross will do anything more than accentuate certain Pekingese characteristics; these would, in any event, shortly disappear if "pure-breeding" were maintained subsequently through a necessary number of generations.

The 1963 Cruft's (British Dog Show) Best of Breed winner was bred from these backcrossed lines, and five out of the six classes were won by dogs of similar breeding. One dog from this line was sold to a Scandinavian breeder, and during the last few years the dog has sired nineteen certificate winners at the Stockholm shows.(In England, dogs are awarded "challenge certificates," commonly called CC's, as the means of achieving championship status).At the Westminster Show in New York, the top three Shih Tzu winners all contained this blood, and other dogs of similar breeding are winning in the Miscellaneous Class throughout the United States.

SHIH TZU STANDARD

By permission of the Kennel Club I am enabled to print the English standard for the Shih Tzu (also used by the A.K.C.):

GENERAL APPEARANCE—Very active, lively and alert, with a distinctly arrogant carriage. The Shih Tzu is neither a terrier nor a toy dog.

HEAD AND SKULL—Head broad and round; wide between the eyes. Shock-headed with hair falling well over the eyes. Good beard and whiskers; the hair growing upwards on the nose gives a distinctly chrysanthemum-like effect. Muzzle square and short, but not wrinkled like a Pekingese; flat and hairy. Nose black from preference and about one inch from tip to top.

EYES—Large, dark and round but not prominent.

EARS—Large, with long leathers, and carried dropping. Set slightly below the crown of the skull; so heavily coated that they appear to blend with the hair of the neck.

MOUTH—Level or slightly underhung.

FOREQUARTERS—Legs short and muscular with ample bone. The legs should look massive on account of the wealth of hair.

BODY—Body between withers and root of tail should be longer than height at withers; well-coupled and sturdy; chest broad and deep, shoulders firm, back level.

HINDQUARTERS—Legs short and muscular with ample bone. They should look straight when viewed from the rear. Thighs well-round and muscular. Legs should look massive on account of the wealth of hair.

FEET—Firm and well padded. They should look big on account of the wealth of hair.

TAIL—Heavily plumed and curled well over back; carried gaily, set on high.

COAT—Long and dense but not curly, with good undercoat.

COLOR—All colors permissible, but a white blaze on forehead and a white tip to the tail are highly prized. Dogs with liver markings may have dark liver noses and slightly lighter eyes. Pigmentation on muzzle as unbroken as possible.

WEIGHT AND SIZE—Up to 18 lb., ideal weight 9-16 lb., type and breed characteristics of the utmost importance and on no account to be sacrificed to size alone.

FAULTS—Narrow heads, big jaws, snipyness, pale pink noses and eye-rims small or light eyes, legginess, sparse coats.

2. Character and Environment

INTELLIGENCE

The Shih Tzu has a great many virtues which cannot fail to make it the small dog of the future. It is not a breed that can live alone in kennels, but one that delights in the society of human beings. Apart from its compact size, its hardiness, soundness, and general good temper, the Shih Tzu is remarkably intelligent. In common with the majority of the short-faced breeds, the brain size is relatively two-and-a-half times that possessed by any of the larger breeds, such as the German Shepherd or the Labrador Retriever. To be perfectly honest one must point out that actual brain weight can be misleading as an index of intelligence; intelligence depends not so much upon quantity as upon quality, and this is dependent upon the structure and complexity of the brain. Nevertheless it is an established

English Champions Pan Wao Chen of Antarctica (left) and Sindi Lu of Antarctica. Judge Bill Jobson presents award to the owner of the champions, Mrs. K. B. Rawlings. Photo by C. M. Cooke and Son.

Three Shih Tzus belonging to Mr. and Mrs. Bill Jobson. From left to right, Sumi San of Darli, Lin Sing of Buddletown, and Ya Mada San of Darli. This line of Shih Tzus is purebred.

fact that the Shih Tzu, in company with the Pekingese, the Pug, the Griffon, and other short-faced breeds does possess a remarkable degree of intelligence. The Shih Tzu does not demonstrate its high intelligence in obedience trials, however, for these tests are, unfortunately, so designed that they inadvertently handicap the Shih Tzu because of its small size, its inability to discriminate between closely allied odors, and the vision-obstructing hair that falls over its eyes.

VISION, BARK

In the matter of vision and ability to discriminate between different scents the Shih Tzu may not be the equal of some of the larger breeds, but it has excellent hearing, and in the way of sense perception, generally, the breed has its own peculiarities and its own mannerisms.

The bark of the breed is also characteristic. There is no noisy yapping, but on special occasions one short, sharp bark which dwindles away into a series of throaty gurgles. It is given to neither expressing nor enjoying noisy outbursts of demonstrative affection, either from its owner or from admiring friends. But it will delight in a country walk and is a hardy, sturdy little dog, slow to wear out, and able to carry on for many years without exhibiting signs of age.

SIZE

It should always be remembered that the Shih Tzu is classed by the English Kennel Club as a "Non-Sporting" dog and *not* a toy dog, so I personally hope that we shall never be allowed to reduce them to toy size. Those who breed specimens that weigh only between six and nine pounds are, I feel, doing the breed an injustice and risking its downfall. Such reduction in size can only lead to difficult whelping (a thing unknown in a normal-size specimen).

In all fairness to breeders of the smaller Shih Tzu, there are and have been a few good specimens, dogs that in spite of their size have been typical, solid, and sound Shih Tzus that have won top honors in England. However, the standard should be foremost in mind.

COLORS

Today there are many varied and beautiful colors in this breed. All colors are permissible. Perhaps the most dramatic and vivid are the well-marked black-and-whites, so much prized if they carry the natty white flash on the head and tail. Breeding for markings is a fascinating job, for one can hope to breed a black with a white flash on its head and tail, four white socks, white undersides, a full white collar round the neck, and with white whiskers to set off that really typical expression.

COATS

According to the standard, which places great emphasis on the coat, the coat can be anything so long as it is not curly. It should be "long and dense," but can be harsh, silky, or fluffy. The only way to get a Shih Tzu into good coat is to regularly brush and comb it; unless the dead hair is removed it will become entangled and matted into the new coat, and the result is a badly groomed dog. The people that present this type of "felted" dog usually try to persuade the judge that it excels in texture and density of coat. It may feel dense, but it doesn't hoodwink the judge who knows the difference between density and neglect! Use a dog shampoo when giving your dog a bath. For detailed advice on the care of claws, teeth, and eyes, see chapter 8, Health.

COAT PREPARATION FOR SHOWS

The best way to show a Shih Tzu is to show it as nature intended: combed, brushed deep down to the skin, and freshly washed. Then one gets the natural coat both for texture and density, and the natural sheen that can be the virtue of every Shih Tzu. I do *not* agree with judges who give top honors to young stock that have not coated up to full length or are still felted up with puppy coat. As we all know, there are the specimens that never coat when adult even though they might carry a reasonable coat at a younger age. If these youngsters are made champions, they may prove poor and worthless champions when mature, because if bred (as they surely will be) they are quite likely to transmit the same type of poor coat. The same comments apply to furnishings on face, tail, legs, and feet. One should judge "on the day" and not on what the dog might be like in a year's time. The Shih Tzu does not reach full beauty or maturity until the age of about three years, and so anything can happen in the meantime.

EXERCISE

Up to the age of six months, puppies need one or two short walks daily on hard roads or pavements. Running on grass spreads the feet and slackens the pasterns and should be avoided. After your Shih Tzu reaches maturity, one brisk walk around the city block will fill your dog's exercise requirements.

FEEDING THE ADULT SHIH TZU

One well-balanced commercial dog food fed toward evening fills the food requirement of the adult Shih Tzu (see chapter 4 for feeding requirements of puppies). As Shih Tzus are small, the cost of providing an adequate diet is minimal. If you buy canned food, study the label carefully and make certain that it contains a large proportion of meat. The lower-priced foods are frequently overloaded with cereal and are low in protein. If you feed dried food, either kibble or meal, add beef fat or bacon grease to bring up the fat content of the diet. To make sure that your dog is getting all the nutrients he needs, buy a diet supplement for him. Your best dog foods will be found at your petshop.

SHELTER

The Shih Tzu is a house pet. Because it is a pet and lives under the same roof as the owner, the breed does not have any geographical limitations. Although your Shih Tzu undoubtedly has the run of the house, a special nook in an out-of-the-way place should be allotted him. This is the area for a comfortable dog bed, either wicker or metal, and toys designed specifically for dogs. Visit your local pet retailer for all of these needs, for it is at the petshop that you will also find the latest in canine clothes to dress up your little canine aristocrat.

3. Faults Found in the Breed Today

TAIL SETS

Although this is only a minor fault, the wrong set of the tail can and does alter the entire outline of the dog.

Low-set tail: this makes the dog appear to have too much fall away behind, and makes it look faultily backed. The dog is unable to plume its tail over its back as required.

Ring tail: this tail is usually set correctly on the body, but the actual formation of the tail is wrong. The end of the tail curls to form a ring, while the main body of the tail fails to fall over the hindquarters into a natural plume.

Flag tail: as seen in hounds. The dog carries this tail far too high, and the outline is presented wrongly. Puppies often carry tails in this way, and allowance should be made for the tail to settle.

Flat tail: here the tail lies flat for its full length on the dog's back. It is usually a very high-set tail that can be carried no other way. This tail gives the impression of a Pomeranian or Pekingese and does not give the desired plume effect.

Side-set tail: a well-plumed tail may be carried to the side of the dog's body. This is wrong despite the true plume's being evident.

Plume tail: this is the one desired in the breed. The tail should be well set on and carried in a plume, the tip of the tail just touching the top line. The hair cascades over the hindquarters and presents the ideal picture of the breed.

Tail sets in the standing dog must be carefully examined during the judging, because the long plumes of hair on the tail can easily be arranged to give the impression that a "wrong set" is right; the faulty set becomes more apparent when the dog is moving. Tail sets must be kept in mind when breeding, because only breeding can produce the right set and formation.

TOP LINES OR BACK

The length of back from withers to root of tail should, as the standard states, be longer than the height at the withers, but here one must use the eye to decide if the dog's look balances in proportion to length of leg and length of back.

When viewed from the side, the top line must appear level. There are varied types of top lines in evidence.

Sway, or broken, back: here the dog's back appears to sag in the middle. The forequarters and the hindquarters appear to be of similar height, but

American Shih Tzu owned by Richard Ball with some of the ribbons and trophies it has won. Photo by Louise Van der Meid.

the middle of the back appears to sag. This is often found in the longer specimens, and may be due to a weaker-than-usual spine. This type of back line often presents "sway" movement, the dog appearing to sway its body in between its legs when on the move.

High at the rear back line: this appears when the hindquarters are higher than the forequarters. The back appears to dip toward the front when the dog is standing, and does not alter from this position when the dog moves. If this stance is seen when the dog is standing, one MUST carefully observe the dog in movement to judge if it is actually higher at the rear end or was simply standing badly at time of the first inspection. Some short-legged breeds may sometimes tuck the hind feet under them when standing, but will move level; of course when the hind legs are slightly pulled out into the natural position this high hindquarter will vanish. If the hindquarters are actually higher, the high rear end will still be apparent when the dog is moving.

Fall-away top line: here we get the dog who is too high in front, the top line falling away to meet low hindquarters. This type of backline is not very often seen; it usually occurs with the "wasp waist" or narrow rear-ended specimen.

Level top line: this is the type to aim at, as it gives the natural line required and usually presents good level and even movement. The dog will appear level all the time.

Left to right: English Ch. Pa Ko of Tiashan, English Ch. Wang Poo of Tiashan, and EE WEE Lam of Tiashan. All are owned by Lady M. Brownrigg.

MOUTH AND JAW PLACEMENTS

Perhaps the first and last parts of a dog ever seen by a judge are the head and face, so this point and its faults must be well considered by the breeder.

The Shih Tzu head and face are distinctive. They must *not* resemble those of a Pekingese, Pug, or terrier-type dog. They should convey an intelligent, lively, and gay expression. Jaw and teeth formation can be either level or slightly underhung. The lips, however, should be level when viewed from the outside.

There are two schools of thought as to whether one should open the mouth or not when judging a Shih Tzu; provided the lips are level when viewed from the outside, the teeth can be of little importance. Shih Tzus, like most other "undershot" small dogs, do not retain their front teeth to advanced age. Therefore those with a few teeth missing in front should not be penalized. If the dog has a full complement of level teeth, so much the better, but if it has a few gaps in the lower jaw, even at an age of two or three years, it should not be considered a poor specimen.

The teeth of English Shih Tzus are not one of the better points of the breed. Even champions may have unlevel, out-of-line teeth, or even missing teeth. This does not matter unduly, provided the jaw set is right. Breeders, however, should see that the first "baby" teeth are removed before the second teeth start to come in. In this way the new teeth have a chance to come in straight without being displaced by the first teeth. It is this displacement, *not* a misformed jaw, that causes the uneven mouth. At times we even find the adult Shih Tzu with two rows of teeth, the first "baby" teeth and a full complement of second teeth. This I feel is a case of too casual attention by the breeder, who should always inspect mouths during development and see that no first teeth remain while the permanent teeth are coming into the gum.

Badly undershot, or "scoop", jaw: a serious fault in the breed. It is not typical, and if the teeth are showing when the mouth is closed, the dog cannot hope to win. Some dogs and bitches have an undershot jaw even to the depth of say a quarter of an inch, yet the lips when closed are level and the specimen can and does win. Again let me point out that it is the closed jaws that matter, not the teeth in particular.

Overshot jaw: an even worse fault than the undershot jaw, but fortunately seldom seen. It occurs in the rather too-long-nosed specimens.

Snipey foreface: here both jaws are level, but the foreface is too narrow and the nose too long; in consequence we have a "snipey" expression, with the true breed characteristics lost. This fault is sometimes coupled with a lower jaw that is too shallow, another serious fault in the breed.

Unless a Shih Tzu has depth to its lower jaw, it fails to have the right foreface and expression. The lack of underjaw tends to give a Pekingese expression, as does the extra flat face (or lack of nose). Both faults seem to combine a wrinkle over the nose as in the Pekingese, and both are serious faults that must be avoided at all costs. The nose of the Shih Tzu should have length (according to size of specimen, not more than an inch for a biggish dog to a good half-inch for a smaller one). It should *not* be a flat nose, and at

Shadza of Chasmu is owned by Mrs. A. Fowler. Photo by Peter Bloomfield.

times we do get a few of these creeping into the breed. The foreface of the Shih Tzu should be level, wide, and balanced, with a good depth and width to the underjaw.

BODY LINES (when viewed from above). The breed calls for a sturdy and solid little dog, and the body must fit. The main faults that we are likely to find seem to be confined to the following:

Wasp waist: here we find the untypical Shih Tzu, a dog wide at the rib and tucked in at the waist, yet with a rear end that would suit a good specimen. This fault is serious, as it gives the Shih Tzu that "Peke" body that the breed is trying to avoid. Wasp waist is often found in Shih Tzus that fail to carry the required amount of hair on the lower fore and hind legs and feet; perhaps this fault is due to the Pekingese cross. The Shih Tzu should have

English Ch. Sumi San of Darli, a black and white bitch, has never gone unplaced at a championship show. She belongs to Mr. and Mrs. Bill Jobson. Photo by Post and Mail.

Shih Tzu puppy Sui Mei owned by Mrs. A. Fowler.
Photo by Peter Bloomfield.

English Ch. Shiraz of Ellingham was bred by Lady Haggerston.
Photo by C. M. Cooke and Son.

heavily furnished legs and feet. On a normal-size specimen of, say, fourteen pounds, it is natural for the dog to carry up to three or three and one-half inches of hair right down the legs and over the feet. Some dogs, however, carry this hair down to the stifle, and then it tapers away to almost nothing; this is wrong.

Narrow rear-ended dogs: this type of Shih Tzu has a good spring of rib frame. This dog will appear to taper away to nothing, which again is foreign to the breed. The ideal is a level muscular little dog, very solid to both feel and see, with no hint of a waist. When lifted it should feel far heavier than one would expect for its size. This latter point also illustrates, I think, why the very small specimens are totally wrong. A Shih Tzu must *not* be a lightweight or easy to carry about. One should think of the Shih Tzu in terms of "light" or "heavy," rather than in terms of "large" or "small," and a good one should always feel heavy regardless of whether it looks large or small.

Because of its long hair, a Shih Tzu may give the impression of having very little length of neck. This is only a delusion, however, and if one could take half a dozen specimens of the breed and measure the distance from the hind part of the skull to the withers, one would find that there are considerable differences between the measurements in the various specimens.

But why is this important? One reason, and a very important one, is that when the neck bones (seven in every dog whether it be a Shih Tzu or a Borzoi) are short, the scapula (shoulder blade bone) lies farther forward, especially at its upper end, with the result that the dog is burdened with what is known as a straight or upright shoulder—one lacking the necessary degree of inclination. Once again, why does this matter? It matters a lot, because a dog with an upright shoulder blade, which goes almost invariably with a short neck, is limited in its forelimb movement. The head is carried low, and there is lessened ability to lift the knee when walking and little inclination to extend the foot forward. Nobody wants a Shih Tzu to step in hackney fashion, as some Poodles are expected to do, but there must be a free swing of the forelimb from the shoulder, sufficient raising of the knee, and a full advancement of the front foot at each stride.

So although your dog may possess all the beauty demanded by the actual standard it may still be incapable of moving gracefully and in a straight line in front; no judge worthy of his salt is going to place your dog over a slightly

American Shih Tzu Gold Ray of Davaar. She was imported from England and is owned by Edith Norton. Photo by Louise Van der Meid.

less-favored animal which is, however, sound and of better conformation than your own. This is where movement comes in. Judges, of course, differ in the degree of importance they attach to movement and soundness over such features as head and coat, and this is why the same dog does not necessarily keep the lead at every show, a circumstance which would soon tend to take the thrill out of showing. The stickler for soundness is more often the all-rounder who may not be so well versed in specialist points, but demands a dog which first and foremost must be sound in body beneath all the trappings of coat, and also one which can stand fairly and squarely on all four feet without help from its handler.

When one examines a dog either as a judge or as a prospective buyer, it is important to stand in front of the animal, behind it, and on either side, and make sure that from each and every one of these positions the body, the limbs, and feet show the degree of squareness or straightness or angulation compatible with soundness in the particular breed to which the dog belongs. Similarly, when watching movement it is equally necessary to study the movement of the feet and limbs from all points of the compass.

Shih Tzus have long been pampered pets. Therefore, provide your Shih Tzu with such necessities as a dogbed (as has been done by Debbie Patterson), special attention, and chewing toys. Photo by Louise Van der Meid.

Winner of the Miscellaneous Dog Class at Chicago's 1963 International was Encore Chopsticks. Breeder and owner is William T. Kibler. Sire, La-Mi Ting Ling; dam, Encore Lovely Lady. Photo by Norman of Chattanooga.

Nor can one estimate the body shape of a hairy dog like a Shih Tzu without using hands, thumbs, and fingers to decide how much of the visible dog is hair and how much is bone and muscle. Never mind the black looks of the handler! We know quite well how much care has gone into getting just that exact set of coat and how annoying it is to see it ruffled, but one must remember that the real dog lies *beneath* the jacket and unless the judge is content to be hoodwinked by the skill of the hairdresser, it is essential to feel and handle the real dog beneath.

FRONTS AND LEGS; MOVEMENT

The feet of a Shih Tzu can be round, oval, or cat-footed, so long as they are firm and well padded. They need not even be big so long as they "look big on account of the wealth of hair."

The Shih Tzu should have a sound tucked-in elbow that gives a very natural front to the dog. The bone should be heavy and solid and with a slight

Richard Ball displays an ideal Shih Tzu carrier for taking this breed to a dog show. Carriers such as these are available at your petshop. Photo by Louise Van der Meid.

bend, not a bow, to the bone. We do not want straight up-and-down "terrier" fronts, but the legs should appear straight and the action should be straight and level when on the move. The most serious faults in the breed are "out at elbow"—wide fronts, and "bowed" bone. Either type of front is wrong and causes a pronounced Pekingese-type roll when moving.

In the Shih Tzu, as in the Old English Sheepdog, a slight roll or swagger, but a well-ordered one which does not interfere with body balance, is not only permissible but favored. The swagger results from a slight "give" in the hock joint, a dropping of the point of the hock (flexion) when weight falls on the hind foot. Nearly every breed possesses its own particular characteristics of gait, but in all breeds (allowing for rolling and exaggerated knee lifting in certain breeds) there are fixed rules which apply as much to Shih Tzus as to Labrador Retrievers or Afghans.

When the dog approaches, the shoulders, elbows and forearms, pasterns, and feet must remain parallel with their opposite numbers, and there must be no punching out of the points of the shoulders or any slackness of the elbows, which must keep close to the sides of the chest. The pasterns from the knee to the feet must turn neither inward nor outward, but must fall perpendicularly to the ground. The weight of the front end of the body must descend upon the appropriate portion of the pads of each foot, and the feet themselves must conform to the type required in the particular breed which the dog represents.

When the dog is going away from the observer, the same remarks apply to stifles and hocks. These must move in parallel with the same parts of the opposite limb, and there must be adequate hock and stifle flexion (the two go together) so that each foot is picked up smartly—revealing the pads to the observer standing behind the dog—and carried smartly forward without the claws skating the ground.

Not all the propulsion comes from the rear end of the dog. The forelimbs do a great deal of the propelling while the head is carried high. It is really only when the head is down, as in hounds and gundogs at work, that the hind limbs take over the greater part of the propulsion of the body. The ability to put this into effect depends upon the shape of the pelvis and the bony development of the loins, quarters, and, particularly, of the second thigh. Unless the loins are strong, well developed, and covered with strong muscles, this matter of hindlimb propulsion cannot be fully exercised.

The Shih Tzu is the most impressive little dog when on the move, going level, soundly, quickly, and straight. It should drive out with reason, give the impression of purpose and arrogance; it should not waddle and should not trip like a toy but, instead, should stride out, flinging its back feet in and out and driving itself along as the active and game dog it is. What we want is a debonair swaggering little canine aristocrat that spells Shih Tzu.

4. The New Puppy

PREPARING FOR THE PUPPY'S ARRIVAL

Because at least three out of four prospective purchasers of dogs want to buy a young rather than an adult or almost adult dog, the problem of preparing for the arrival of a permanent canine house guest almost always means preparing for the arrival of a puppy. This is not to say that there is anything wrong with purchasing an adult dog; on the contrary, such a purchase has definite advantages in that it often allows freedom from housebreaking chores and rigorous feeding schedules, and these are of definite benefit to prospective purchasers who have little time to spare. Since the great majority of dog buyers, however, prefer to watch their pet grow from sprawlingly playful puppyhood to dignified maturity, buying a dog, practically speaking, means buying a puppy.

Before you get a puppy be sure that you are willing to take the responsibility of training him and caring for his physical needs. His early training is most important, as an adult dog that is a well-behaved member of the family is the end product of your early training. Remember that your new puppy knows only a life of romping with his littermates and the security of being with his mother, and that coming into your home is a new and sometimes frightening experience for him. He will adjust quickly if you are patient with him and show him what you expect of him. If there are small children in the family be sure that they do not abuse him or play roughly with him. A puppy plays hard, but he also requires frequent periods of rest. Before he comes, decide where he is to sleep and where he is to eat. If your puppy does not have a collar, find out the size he requires and buy an inexpensive one, as he will soon outgrow it. Have the proper grooming equipment on hand. Consult the person from whom you bought the puppy as to the proper food for your puppy, and learn the feeding time and amount that he eats a day. Buy him some toys—usually the breeder will give you some particular toy or toys which he has cherished as a puppy to add to his new ones and to make him less homesick. Get everything you need from your petshop *before* you bring the puppy home.

MALE OR FEMALE?

Before buying your puppy you should have made a decision as to whether you want a male or a female. Unless you want to breed your pet and raise a litter of puppies, your preference as to the sex of your puppy is strictly a personal choice. Both sexes are pretty much the same in disposition and character, and both make equally good pets.

WHERE TO BUY YOUR PUPPY

Although petshop owners are necessarily restricted from carrying all breeds in stock, they know the best dog breeders and are sometimes able to supply quality puppies on demand. In cases in which a petshop owner is unable to obtain a dog for you, he can still refer you to a good source, such as a reputable kennel. If your local petshop proprietor is unable to either obtain a dog for you or refer you to someone from whom you can purchase one, don't give up: there are other avenues to explore. The American Kennel Club will furnish you addresses. Additional sources of information are the various magazines devoted to the dog fancy.

SIGNS OF GOOD HEALTH

Picking out a healthy, attractive little fellow to join the family circle is a different matter from picking a show dog; it is also a great deal less complicated. Often the puppy will pick you. If he does, and it is mutual admiration at first sight, he is the best puppy for you. At a reliable kennel or petshop the owner will be glad to answer your questions and to point out the difference between pet and show-quality puppies. Trust your eyes and hands to tell if the puppies are sound in body and temperament. Ears and eyes should not have suspicious discharges. Legs should have strong bones; bodies should have solid muscles. Coats should be clean. Lift the hair to see if the skin is free of scales and parasites.

Temperament can vary from puppy to puppy in the same litter. There is always one puppy which will impress you by his energy and personality. He loves to show off and will fling himself all over you and his littermates, and everyone who comes to see the puppies falls in love with him. However, do not overlook the more reserved puppy. Most dogs are wary of strangers, so reserve may indicate caution, not a timid puppy. He may calmly accept your presence when he senses that all is well. Such a puppy should be a steady reliable dog when mature. In any event, never force yourself on a puppy — let him come to you. Reliable breeders and petshops will urge you to take your puppy to the veterinarian of your choice to have the puppy's health checked, and will allow you at least two days in which to have it done. It should be clearly understood whether rejection by a veterinarian for health reasons means that you have the choice of another puppy from that litter or that you get your money back.

AGE AT WHICH PUPPY SHOULD BE PURCHASED

A puppy should be at least six weeks of age before you take him home. Many breeders will not let puppies go before they are two months old. In general, the puppy you buy for show and breeding should be five or six months old. If you want a show dog, remember that not even an expert can predict with 100% accuracy what a small puppy will be when he grows up.

PAPERS

When you buy a purebred dog you should receive his American Kennel Club registration certificate (or an application form to fill out), a pedigree, and a health certificate made out by the breeder's veterinarian. The registration certificate is the official A.K.C. paper. If the puppy was named and registered by his breeder you will want to complete the transfer and send it, with the fee, to the American Kennel Club. They will transfer the dog to your ownership in their records and send a new certificate to you. If you receive, instead, an application for registration, you should fill it out, choosing a name for your dog, and mail it, with the fee, to the A.K.C.

The pedigree is a chart showing your puppy's ancestry and is not a part of his official papers. The health certificate will tell what shots have been given and when the next ones are due. Your veterinarian will be appreciative of this information, and will continue with the same series of shots if they have not been completed. The health certificate will also give the dates on which the puppy has been wormed. Ask your veterinarian whether rabies shots are required in your locality. Most breeders will give you food for a few days along with instructions for feeding so that your puppy will have the same diet he is accustomed to until you can buy a supply at your petshop.

THE PUPPY'S FIRST NIGHT WITH YOU

The puppy's first night at home is likely to be disturbing to the family. Keep in mind that suddenly being away from his mother, brothers, and sisters is a new experience for him; he may be confused and frightened. If you have a special room in which you have his bed, be sure that there is nothing there with which he can harm himself. Be sure that all lamp cords are out of his reach and that there is nothing that he can tip or pull over. Check furniture that he might get stuck under or behind and objects that he might chew. If you want him to sleep in your room he probably will be quiet all night, reassured by your presence. If left in a room by himself he will cry and howl, and you will have to steel yourself to be impervious to his whining. After a few nights alone he will adjust. The first night that he is alone it is wise to put a loud-ticking alarm clock, as well as his toys, in the room with him. The alarm clock will make a comforting noise, and he will not feel that he is alone.

YOUR PUPPY'S BED

Every dog likes to have a place that is his alone. He holds nothing more sacred than his own bed whether it be a rug, dog crate, or dog bed. If you get your puppy a bed be sure to get one which discourages chewing. Also be sure that the bed is large enough to be comfortable for him when he is fully grown. Locate it away from drafts and radiators. A word might be said here in defense of the crate, which many pet owners think is cruel and confining. Given a choice, a young dog instinctively selects a secure place

Special dog feeding and watering utensils are so designed as to safeguard your pet from dangerous porcelain chips. These utensils are easy to keep clean, too.

in which to lounge, rest, or sleep. The walls and ceiling of a crate, even a wire one, answer that need. Once he regards his crate as a safe and reassuring place to stay, you will be able to leave him alone in the house.

FEEDING YOUR PUPPY

As a general rule, a puppy from weaning time (six weeks) to three months of age should have *four meals a day;* from three months to six months, *three meals;* from six months to one year, *two meals.* After a year, a dog does well on *one meal daily.* There are as many feeding schedules as there are breeders, and puppies do fine on all of them, so it is best for the new owner to follow the one given him by the breeder of his puppy. Remember that all dogs are individuals. The amount that will keep your dog in good health is right for him, not the "rule-book" amount. A feeding schedule to give you some idea of what the average puppy will eat is as follows:

Morning meal:	Puppy meal with milk.
Afternoon meal:	Meat mixed with puppy meal, plus a vitamin-mineral supplement.
Evening meal:	Same as afternoon meal, but without a vitamin-mineral supplement.

Do not change the amounts in your puppy's diet too rapidly. If he gets diarrhea it may be that he is eating too much, so cut back on his food and when he is normal again increase his food more slowly.

There is a canned food made especially for puppies which you can buy only by a veterinarian's prescription. Some breeders use this very successfully from weaning to three months.

TRANSITIONAL DIET

Changing over to an adult program of feeding is not difficult. Very often the puppy will change himself; that is, he will refuse to eat some of his meals. He adjusts to his one meal (or two meals) a day without any trouble at all.

BREAKING TO COLLAR AND LEASH

Puppies are usually broken to a collar before you bring them home, but even if yours has never worn one it is a simple matter to get him used to it. Put a loose collar on him for a few hours at a time. At first he may scratch at it and try to get it off, but gradually he will take it as a matter of course. To break him to a lead, attach his leash to his collar and let him drag it around. When he becomes used to it pick it up and gently pull him in the direction you want him to go. He will think it is a game, and with a bit of patience on your part he will allow himself to be led.

DISCIPLINING YOUR PUPPY

The way to have a well-mannered adult dog is to give him firm basic training while he is a puppy. When you say "No" you must mean "No." Your dog will respect you only if you are firm. A six- to eight-weeks-old puppy is old enough to understand what "No" means. The first time you see your puppy doing something he shouldn't be doing, chewing something he shouldn't chew, or wandering in a forbidden area, it's time to teach him. Shout, "No." Puppies do not like loud noises, and your misbehaving pet will readily connect the word with something unpleasant. Usually a firm "No" in a disapproving tone of voice is enough to correct your dog, but occasionally you get a puppy that requires a firmer hand, especially as he grows older. In this case hold your puppy firmly and slap him gently across the hindquarters. If this seems cruel, you should realize that no dog resents being disciplined if he is caught in the act of doing something wrong, and your puppy will be intelligent enough to know what the slap was for.

After you have slapped him and you can see that he has learned his lesson, call him to you and talk to him in a pleasant tone of voice — praise him for coming to you. This sounds contradictory, but it works with a puppy. He immediately forgives you, practically tells you that it was his fault and that he deserved his punishment, and promises that it will not happen again. This form of discipline works best and may be used for all misbehaviors.

Never punish your puppy by chasing him around, making occasional swipes with a rolled-up newspaper; punish him only when you have a firm hold on him. Above all, never punish your dog after having called him to you. He must learn to associate coming to you with something pleasant.

HOUSEBREAKING

While housebreaking your puppy do not let him have the run of the house. If you do you will find that he will pick out his own bathroom, which may be in your bedroom or in the middle of the living room rug. Keep him confined to a small area where you can watch him, and you will be able to train him much more easily and speedily. A puppy does not want to dirty his bed, but he does need to be taught where he should go. Spread papers over his living quarters, then watch him carefully. When you notice him starting to whimper, sniff the floor, or run agitatedly in little circles, rush him to the place that you want to serve as his relief area and gently hold him there until he relieves himself. Then praise him lavishly. When you remove the soiled papers, leave a small damp piece so that the puppy's sense of smell will lead him back there next time. If he makes a mistake, wash the area at once with warm water, followed by a rinse with water and vinegar or sudsy ammonia. This will kill the odor and prevent discoloration. It shouldn't take more than a few days for him to get the idea of using newspapers. When he becomes fairly consistent, reduce the area of paper to a few sheets in a corner. As soon as you think he has the idea fixed in his mind, you can let him roam around the house a bit, but keep an eye on him. It might be best to keep him on leash the first few days so that you can rush him back to his paper at any signs of an approaching accident.

The normal healthy puppy will want to relieve himself when he wakes up in the morning, after each feeding, and after strenuous exercise. During early puppyhood any excitement, such as the return home of a member of the family or the approach of a visitor, may result in floor-wetting, but that phase should pass in a few weeks. Keep in mind that you can't expect too much from your puppy until he is about five months old. Before that, his muscles and digestive system just aren't under his control.

OUTDOOR HOUSEBREAKING

You can begin outdoor training on leash even while you are paper-training your puppy. First thing in the morning take him outdoors (to the curb, if you are in the city) and walk him back and forth in a small area until he relieves himself. He will probably make a puddle and then walk around, uncertain of what is expected of him. You can try standing him over a newspaper, which may give him the idea. Some dog trainers use glycerine suppositories at this point for fast action. Praise your dog every time taking him outside brings results, and he will get the idea. You'll find, when you begin the outdoor training, that the male puppy usually requires a longer walk than the female. Both male and female puppies will squat. It isn't until he is older that the male dog will begin to lift his leg. If you hate to give up your sleep, you can train your puppy to go outdoors during the day and use the paper at night.

5. Training

WHEN TO START TRAINING

You should never begin SERIOUS obedience training before your dog is seven or eight months old. (Some animal psychologists state that puppies can begin training when seven weeks old, if certain techniques are followed. These techniques, however, are still experimental and should be left to the professional trainer to prove their worth.) While your dog is still in his early puppyhood, concentrate on winning his confidence so he will love and admire you. This will make his training easier, since he will do anything to please you. Basic training can be started at the age of three or four months. He should be taught to walk nicely on a leash, sit and lie down on command, and come when he is called.

YOUR PART IN TRAINING

You must patiently demonstrate to your dog what each word of command means. Guide him with your hands and the training leash, reassuring him with your voice, through whatever routine you are teaching him. Repeat the word associated with the act. Demonstrate again and again to give the dog a chance to make the connection in his mind.

Once he begins to get the idea, use the word of command without any physical guidance. Drill him. When he makes mistakes, correct him, kindly at first, more severely as his training progresses. Try not to lose your patience or become irritated, and never slap him with your hand or the leash during the training session. Withholding praise or rebuking him will make him feel bad enough.

When he does what you want, praise him lavishly with words and with pats. Don't continually reward with dog candy or treats in training. The dog that gets into the habit of performing for a treat will seldom be fully dependable when he can't smell or see one in the offing. When he carries out a command, even though his performance is slow or sloppy, praise him and he will perform more readily the next time.

THE TRAINING VOICE

When you start training your dog, use your training voice, giving commands in a firm, clear tone. Once you give a command, persist until it is obeyed, even if you have to pull the dog to obey you. He must learn that training is different from playing, that a command once given must be obeyed no matter what distractions are present. Remember that the tone and pitch of your voice, not loudness, are the qualities that will influence your dog most.

Be consistent in the use of words during training. Confine your commands to as few words as possible and never change them. It is best for only one person to carry on the dog's training, because different people will use different words and tactics that will confuse your dog. The dog who hears *"come,"* *"get over here,"* *"hurry up,"* *"here, Rex,"* and other commands when he is wanted will become totally confused.

TRAINING LESSONS

Training is hard on the dog — and on the trainer. A young dog just cannot take more than ten minutes of training at a stretch, so limit the length of your first lessons. Then you can gradually increase the length of time to about thirty minutes. You'll find that you too will tend to become impatient when you stretch out a training lesson. If you find yourself losing your temper, stop and resume the lesson at another time. Before and after each lesson have a play period, but don't play during a training session. Even the youngest dog soon learns that schooling is a serious matter; fun comes afterward.

Don't spend too much time on one phase of the training, or the dog will become bored. Always try to end a lesson on a pleasant note. Actually, in nine cases out of ten, if your dog isn't doing what you want it's because you're not getting the idea over to him properly.

YOUR TRAINING EQUIPMENT AND ITS USE

The leash is more properly called the lead, so we'll use that term here. The best leads for training are the six-foot webbed-cloth leads, usually olive-drab in color, and the six-foot leather lead. Fancier leads are available and may be used if desired.

You'll need a metal-link collar, called a choke chain, consisting of a metal chain with rings on each end. Even though the name may sound frightening, it won't hurt your dog, and it is an absolute MUST in training. There is a right and a wrong way to put the training collar on. It should go around the dog's neck so that you can attach the lead to the ring at the end of the chain which passes OVER, not under his neck. It is most important that the collar is put on properly so it will tighten when the lead is pulled and ease when you relax your grip.

The correct way to hold the lead is also very important, as the collar should have some slack in it, at all times, except when correcting. Holding the loop in your right hand, extend your arm out to the side, even with your shoulder. With your left hand, grasp the lead as close as possible to the collar, without making it tight. The remaining portion of the lead can be made into a loop which is held in the right hand. Keep this arm close to your body. Most corrections will be made with the left hand by giving the lead a jerk in the direction you want the dog to go. The dog that pulls and forges ahead can be corrected by a steady pull on the lead.

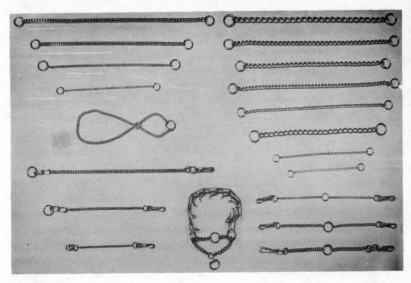

Special training collars for your dog can be purchased at your petshop.

HEELING

"*Heeling*" in dog language means having your dog walk alongside you on your left side, close to your leg, on lead or off. With patience and effort you can train your dog to walk with you even on a crowded street or in the presence of other dogs.

Now that you have learned the correct way to put on your dog's collar and how to hold the lead, you are ready to start with his first lesson in heeling. Put the dog at your left side, sitting. Using the dog's name and the command "*Heel*," start forward on your LEFT foot, giving a tug on the lead to get the dog started. Always use the dog's name first, followed by the command, such as "*Rex, heel*." Saying his name will help get his attention and will let him know that you are about to give a command.

Walk briskly, with even steps, going around in a large circle, square, or straight line. While walking, make sure that your dog stays on the left side and close to your leg. If he lags behind, give several tugs on the lead to get him up to you, then praise him for doing well. If he forges ahead or swings wide, stop and jerk the lead sharply and bring him back to the proper position. Always repeat the command when correcting, and praise him when he does well. If your dog continues to pull or lag behind, either your corrections are not severe enough or your timing between correction and praise is off. Do this exercise for only five minutes at first, gradually lengthening it to fifteen, or even half an hour.

To keep your dog's attention, talk to him as you keep him in place. You can also do a series of fast about-turns, giving the lead a jerk as you turn. He will gradually learn that he must pay attention or be jerked to your side. You can vary the routine by changing speeds, doing turns, figure-eights, and by zig-zagging across the training area.

"HEEL" MEANS "SIT," TOO

To the dog, the command *"Heel"* will also mean that he has to sit in the heel position at your left side when you stop walking — with no additional command from you. As you practice heeling, make him sit whenever you stop, at first using the word *"Sit,"* then with no command at all. He'll soon get the idea and sit down when you stop and wait for the command *"Heel"* to start walking again.

TRAINING TO SIT

Training your dog to sit should be fairly easy. Stand him on your left side, holding the lead fairly short, and command him to *"Sit."* As you give the verbal command, pull up slightly with the lead and push his hindquarters down. Do not let him lie down or stand up. Keep him in a sitting position for a moment, then release the pressure on the lead and praise him. Constantly repeat the command as you hold him in a sitting position, thus fitting the word to the action in his mind. After a while he will begin to get the idea and will sit without your having to push his hindquarters down. When he reaches that stage, insist that he sit on command. If he is slow to obey, slap his hindquarters with your hand to get him down fast. *DO NOT HIT HIM HARD!* Teach him to sit on command facing you as well as when he is at your side. When he begins sitting on command with the lead on, try it with the lead off.

THE "LIE DOWN"

The object of this is to get the dog to lie down either on the verbal command *"Down"* or when you give him the hand signal, your hand raised in front of you, palm down. This is one of the most important parts of training. A well-trained dog will drop on command and stay down whatever the temptation: cat-chasing, car-chasing, or another dog across the street.

Don't start training to lie down until the dog is almost letter-perfect in sitting on command. Then place the dog in a sit, and kneel before him. With both hands, reach forward to his legs and take one front leg in each hand, thumbs up, and holding just below his elbows. Lift his legs slightly off the ground and pull them somewhat out in front of him. Simultaneously, give the command *"Down"* and lower his front legs to the ground.

Hold the dog down and stroke him to let him know that staying down is what you want him to do. This method is far better than forcing a young dog down. Using force can cause him to become very frightened and he will begin to dislike any training. Always talk to your dog and let him know that you are very pleased with him, and soon you will find that you have a happy working dog.

After he begins to get the idea, slide the lead under your left foot and give the command "*Down*." At the same time, pull the lead. This will help get the dog down. Meanwhile, raise your hand in the down signal. Don't expect to accomplish all this in one session. Be patient and work with the dog. He'll cooperate if you show him just what you expect him to do.

THE "STAY"

The next step is to train your dog to stay either in a "*Sit*" or "*Down*" position. Sit him at your side. Give the command "*Stay*," but be careful not to use his name with this command, because hearing his name may lead him to think that some action is expected of him. If he begins to move, repeat "*Stay*" firmly and hold him down in the sit. Constantly repeat the word "*Stay*" to fix the meaning of that command in his mind. After he has learned to stay for a short time, gradually increase the length of his stay. The hand signal for the stay is a downward sweep of your hand toward the dog's nose, with the palm facing him. While he is sitting, walk around him and stand in front of him. Hold the lead at first; later, drop the lead on the ground in front of him and keep him sitting. If he bolts, scold him and place him back in the same position, repeating the command and all the exercise.

Use some word such as "*Okay*" or "*Up*" to let him know when he can get up, and praise him well for a good performance. As this practice continues, walk farther and farther away from him. Later, try sitting him, giving the command to stay, and then walk out of sight, first for a few seconds, then for longer periods. A well-trained dog should stay where you put him without moving until you come and release him.

Similarly, practice having him stay in the down position, first with you near him, later when you step out of sight.

THE "COME" ON COMMAND

You can train your dog to come when you call him, if you begin when he is young. At first, work with him on lead. Sit the dog, then back away the length of the lead and call him, putting into your voice as much coaxing affection as possible. Give an easy tug on the lead to get him started. When he does come, make a big fuss over him; it might help at this point to give him a small piece of dog candy or food as a reward. He should get the idea soon. You can also move away from him the full length of the lead and call to him something like "*Rex, come*," then run backward a few steps and stop, making him sit directly in front of you.

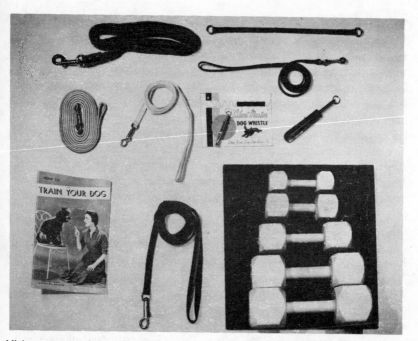

Visit your petshop for all of the training equipment you will need to make your pet a better canine citizen.

Don't be too eager to practice coming on command off lead. Wait until you are certain that you have the dog under perfect control before you try calling him when he's free. Once he gets the idea that he can disobey a command and get away with it, your training program will suffer a serious setback. Keep in mind that your dog's life may depend on his immediate response to a command to come when he is called. If he disobeys off lead, put the lead back on and correct him severely with jerks of the lead.

TEACHING TO COME TO HEEL

The object of this is for you to stand still, say "*Heel*," and have your dog come right over to you and sit by your left knee in the heel position. If your dog has been trained to sit without command every time you stop, he's ready for this step.

Sit him in front of and facing you and step back one step. Moving only your left foot, pull the dog behind you, then step forward and pull him around until he is in a heel position. You can also have the dog go around by passing the lead behind your back. Use your left heel to straighten him out if he begins to sit behind you or crookedly. This may take a little work, but he will get the idea if you show him just what you want.

THE "STAND"

Your dog should be trained to stand in one spot without moving his feet, and he should allow a stranger to run his hand over his body and legs without showing any resentment or fear. Employ the same method you used in training him to stay on the sit and down. While walking, place your left hand out, palm toward his nose, and command him to stay. His first impulse will be to sit, so be prepared to stop him by placing your hand under his body, near his hindquarters, and holding him until he gets the idea that this is different from the command to sit. Praise him for standing, then walk to the end of the lead. Correct him strongly if he starts to move. Have a stranger approach him and run his hands over the dog's back and down his legs. Keep him standing until you come back to him. Walk around him from his left side, come to the heel position, and make sure that he does not sit until you command him to.

This is a very valuable exercise. If you plan to show your dog he will have learned to stand in a show pose and will allow the judge to examine him.

TRAINING SCHOOLS AND CLASSES

There are dog-training classes in all parts of the country, some sponsored by the local humane society.

If you feel that you lack the time or the skill to train your dog yourself, there are professional dog trainers who will do it for you, but basically dog training is a matter of training YOU and your dog to work together as a team, and if you don't do it yourself you will miss a lot of fun. Don't give up after trying unsuccessfully for a short time. Try a little harder and you and your dog will be able to work things out.

ADVANCED TRAINING AND OBEDIENCE TRIALS

Once you begin training your dog and you see how well he does, you'll probably be bitten by the "obedience bug" — the desire to enter him in obedience trials held under American Kennel Club auspices.

The A.K.C. obedience trials are divided into three classes: Novice, Open, and Utility.

In the Novice Class, the dog will be judged on the following basis:

TEST	MAXIMUM SCORE
Heel on lead	35
Stand for examination	30
Heel free — off lead	45
Recall (come on command)	30
One-minute sit (handler in ring)	30
Three-minute down (handler in ring)	30
Maximum total score	200

If the dog "qualifies" in three shows by earning at least 50% of the points for each test, with a total of at least 170 for the trial, he has earned the Companion Dog degree and the letters C.D. (Companion Dog) are entered after his name in the A.K.C. records.

After the dog has qualified as a C.D., he is eligible to enter the Open Class competition, where he will be judged on this basis:

TEST	MAXIMUM SCORE
Heel free	40
Drop on Recall	30
Retrieve (wooden dumbbell) on flat	25
Retrieve over obstacle (hurdle)	35
Broad jump	20
Three-minute sit (handler out of ring)	25
Five-minute down (handler out of ring)	25
Maximum total score	200

Again he must qualify in three shows for the C.D.X. (Companion Dog Excellent) title and then is eligible for the Utility Class, where he can earn the Utility Dog (U.D.) degree in these rugged tests:

TEST	MAXIMUM SCORE
Scent discrimination (picking up article handled by master from group) Article 1	20
Scent discrimination Article 2	20
Scent discrimination Article 3	20
Seek back (picking up an article dropped by handler)	30
Signal exercise (heeling, etc., on hand signal)	35
Directed jumping (over hurdle and bar jump)	40
Group examination	35
Maximum total score	200

For more complete information about these obedience trials, write for the American Kennel Club's *Regulations and Standards for Obedience Trials*. Dogs that are disqualified from breed shows because of alteration or physical defects are eligible to compete in these trials. Besides the formal A.K.C. obedience trials, there are informal "match" shows in which dogs compete for ribbons and inexpensive trophies. These shows are run by many local fanciers' dog clubs and by all-breed obedience clubs. In many localities the humane society and other groups conduct their own obedience shows. Your local petshop or kennel can keep you informed about such shows in your vicinity, and you will find them listed in the different dog magazines or in the pet column of your local newspaper.

6. Breeding

THE QUESTION OF SPAYING

If you feel that you will never want to raise a litter of purebred puppies, and if you do not wish to risk the possibility of an undesirable mating and surplus mongrel puppies inevitably destined for execution at the local pound, you may want to have your female spayed. Spaying is generally best performed after the female has passed her first heat and before her first birthday: this allows the female to attain the normal female characteristics, while still being young enough to avoid the possible complications encountered when an older female is spayed. A spayed female will remain a healthy, lively pet. You often hear that an altered female will become very fat. However, if you cut down on her food intake, she will not gain weight.

On the other hand, if you wish to show your dog (altered females are disqualified) or enjoy the excitement and feeling of accomplishment of breeding and raising a litter of puppies, particularly in your breed and from your pet, then definitely do not spay.

Male dogs, unlike tomcats, are almost never altered (castrated).

SEXUAL PHYSIOLOGY

Females usually reach sexual maturity (indicated by the first heat cycle, or season) at eight or nine months of age, but sexual maturity may occur as early as six months or as late as thirteen months of age. The average heat cycle (estrus period) lasts for twenty or twenty-one days, and occurs approximately every six months. For about five days immediately preceding the heat period, the female generally displays restlessness and an increased appetite. The vulva, or external genitals, begin to swell. The discharge, which is bright red at the onset and gradually becomes pale pink to straw in color, increases in quantity for several days and then slowly subsides, finally ceasing altogether. The vaginal discharge is subject to much variation: in some bitches it is quite heavy, in others it may never appear, and in some it may be so slight as to go unnoticed.

About eight or nine days after the first appearance of the discharge, the female becomes very playful with other dogs, but will not allow a mating to take place. Anywhere from the tenth or eleventh day, when the discharge has virtually ended and the vulva has softened, to the seventeenth or eighteenth day, the female will accept males and be able to conceive. Many biologists apply the term "heat" only to this receptive phase rather than to the whole estrus, as is commonly done by dog fanciers.

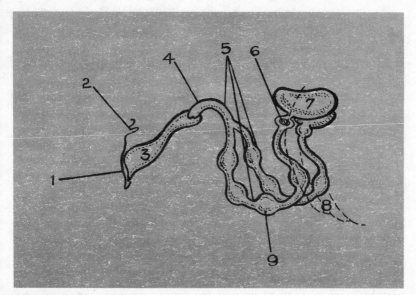

The reproduction system of the bitch: 1, vulva; 2, anus; 3, vagina; 4, cervix; 5, uterus; 6, ovary; 7, kidneys; 8, ribs; 9, fetal lump.

The ova (egg cells) from the female's ovaries are discharged into the oviduct toward the close of the acceptance phase, usually from the sixteenth to eighteenth day. From the eighteenth day until the end of the cycle, the female is still attractive to males, but she will repulse their advances. The entire estrus, however, may be quite variable: in some females vaginal bleeding ends and mating begins on the fourth day; in others, the discharge may continue throughout the entire cycle and the female will not accept males until the seventeenth day or even later.

The male dog — simply referred to by fanciers as the "dog," in contrast to the female, which is referred to as the "bitch" — upon reaching sexual maturity, usually at about six to eight months, is able, like other domesticated mammals, to breed at any time throughout the year.

The testes, the sperm-producing organs of the male, descend from the body cavity into the scrotum at birth. The condition of *cryptorchidism* refers to the retention of one or both testes within the body cavity. A testicle retained within the body cavity is in an environment too hot for it to function normally. A retained testicle may also become cancerous. If only one testicle descends, the dog is known as a *monorchid;* if neither descends, the dog is known as an *anorchid* (dog fanciers, however, refer to a dog with the latter condition as a cryptorchid). A monorchid dog is a fertile animal; an anorchid is sterile.

The male dog's penis has a bulbous enlargement at its base and, in addition, like the penis of a number of other mammals, contains a bone. When mating occurs, pressure on the penis causes a reflex action that fills the bulb with blood, swelling it to about five times its normal size within the female. This locks, or ties, the two animals together. After ejaculation, the animals usually remain tied for fifteen to thirty minutes, but they may separate very quickly or remain together an hour or more, depending on the length of time it takes for the blood to drain from the bulb.

CARE OF THE FEMALE IN ESTRUS

If you have a dog-proof run within your yard, it will be safe to leave your female in season there; if you don't have such a run, she should be shut indoors. Don't leave her alone outside even for a minute; she should be exercised only on lead. If you want to prevent the neighborhood dogs from congregating around your doorstep, as they inevitably will as soon as they discover that your female is in season, take her some distance from the house before you let her relieve herself. Take her in your car to a park or field for a chance to "stretch" her legs (always on lead of course). Keep watch for male dogs, and if one approaches take the female back to the car. After the three weeks are up you can let her out as before with no worry that she can have puppies until her next season.

Some owners find it simpler to board their female at a kennel until her season is over. However, it really is not difficult to watch your female at home. There are various products on the market which are useful at this time. Although the female in season keeps herself quite clean, sometimes she unavoidably stains furniture or rugs. You can buy sanitary belts made especially for dogs at your petshop. Consult your veterinarian for information on pills to be taken to check odor during this period. There also is a pill that prevents the female from coming in season for extended periods, and there are many different types of liquids, powders, and sprays of varying efficiency used to keep male dogs away. However, the one safe rule (whatever products you use) is: keep your bitch away from dogs that could mount her.

SHOULD YOU BREED YOUR MALE?

As with every question, whether or not to use a male dog as a stud has two sides. The arguments for and against using a dog as a stud are often very close to the ridiculous. A classic example would be the tale that once you use a dog as a stud he will lose his value as a show dog or any one of the other functions a dog may have. A sound rule may well be: *if you have a stud who has proven his worth at the shows, place his services out for hire, if only for the betterment of the breed; if your dog is not of show quality, do not use him as a stud.*

Top champion studs can bring their owners many dollars in breeding revenue. If the stud is as good as you feel he is, his services will soon be in great demand. Using a dog as a stud will not lower his value in other functions in any way. Many breeders will permit a male dog to breed an experienced female once, when about a year old, and then they begin to show their stud until he has gained his conformation championship. He is then placed out for hire through advertising in the various bulletins, journals, and show catalogs, and through the stud registers maintained by many pet-shops.

SHOULD YOU BREED YOUR FEMALE?

If you are an amateur and decide to breed your female it would be wise to talk with a breeder and find out all that breeding and caring for puppies entails. You must be prepared to assume the responsibility of caring for the mother through her pregnancy and for the puppies until they are of saleable age. Raising a litter of puppies can be a rewarding experience, but it means work as well as fun, and there is no guarantee of financial profit. As the puppies grow older and require more room and care, the amateur breeder, in desperation, often sells the puppies for much less than they are worth; sometimes he has to give them away. If the cost of keeping the puppies will drain your finances, think twice.

If you have given careful consideration to all these things and still want to breed your female, remember that there is some preparation necessary before taking this step.

WHEN TO BREED

It is usually best to breed in the second or third season. Consider when the puppies will be born and whether their birth and later care will inter-fere with your work or vacation plans. Gestation period is approximately fifty-eight to sixty-three days. Allow enough time to select the right stud for her. Don't be in a position of having to settle for any available male if she comes into season sooner than expected. Your female will probably be ready to breed twelve days after the first colored discharge. You can usually make arrangements to board her with the owner of the male for a few days to insure her being there at the proper time, or you can take her to be mated and bring her home the same day. If she still appears receptive she may be bred again a day or two later. Some females never show signs of willingness, so it helps to have the experience of a breeder. The second day after the discharge changes color is the proper time; she may be bred for about three days following. For an additional week or so she may have some discharge and attract other dogs by her odor, but she can seldom be bred at this time.

HOW TO SELECT A STUD

Choose a mate for your female with an eye to countering her deficiencies. If possible, both male and female should have several ancestors in common within the last two or three generations, as such combinations generally "click" best. The male should have a good show record himself or be the sire of champions. The owner of the stud usually charges a fee for the use of the dog. The fee varies. Payment of a fee does not guarantee a litter, but it does generally confer the right to breed your female again to the stud if she does not have puppies the first time. In some cases the owner of the stud will agree to take a choice puppy in place of a stud fee. You and the owner of the stud should settle all details beforehand, including such questions as what age the puppies should reach before the stud's owner can make his choice, what disposition is made of a single surviving puppy under an agreement by which the stud owner has pick of the litter, and so on. In all cases it is best that the agreement entered into by bitch owner and stud owner be in the form of a written contract.

It is customary for the female to be sent to the male; if the stud dog of your choice lives any distance you will have to make arrangements to have your female shipped to him. The quickest way is by air, and if you call your nearest airport the airline people will give you information as to the best and fastest flight. Some airlines furnish their own crates for shipping, whereas others require that you furnish your own. The owner of the stud will make the arrangements for shipping the female back to you. You have to pay all shipping charges.

PREPARATION FOR BREEDING

Before you breed your female, make sure she is in good health. She should be neither too thin nor too fat. Skin diseases must be cured before breeding; a bitch with skin diseases can pass them on to her puppies. If she has worms she should be wormed before being bred, or within three weeks afterward. It is a good idea to have your veterinarian give her a booster shot for distemper and hepatitis before the puppies are born. This will increase the immunity the puppies receive during their early, most vulnerable period. Choose a dependable veterinarian and rely on him if there is an emergency when your female whelps.

HOW OFTEN SHOULD YOU BREED YOUR FEMALE?

Do not breed your bitch after she reaches six years of age. If you wish to breed her several times while she is young, it is wise to breed her only once a year. In other words, breed her, skip a season, and then breed her again. This will allow her to gain back her full strength between whelpings.

THE IMPORTANCE AND APPLICATION OF GENETICS

Any person attempting to breed dogs should have a basic understanding of the transmission of traits, or characteristics, from the parents to the offspring and some familiarity with the more widely used genetic terms that he will probably encounter. A knowledge of the fundamental mechanics of genetics enables a breeder to better comprehend the passing, complementing, and covering of both good points and faults from generation to generation. It enables him to make a more judicial and scientific decision in selecting potential mates.

Inheritance, fundamentally, is due to the existence of microscopic units, known as *GENES*, present in the cells of all individuals. Genes somehow control the biochemical reactions that occur within the embryo or adult organism. This control results in changing or guiding the development of the organism's characteristics. A "string" of attached genes is known as a *CHROMOSOME*. With a few important exceptions, every chromosome has a partner chromosome carrying a duplicate or equivalent set of genes. Each gene, therefore, has a partner gene, known as an *ALLELE*. The number of different pairs of chromosomes present in the cells of the organism varies with the type of organism: a certain parasitic worm has only one pair, a certain fruit fly has four different pairs, man has 23 different pairs, and your dog has 39 different pairs per cell. Because each chromosome may have many hundreds of genes, a single cell of the body may contain a total of several thousand genes. Heredity is obviously a very complex matter.

In the simplest form of genetic inheritance, one particular gene and its duplicate, or allele, on the partner chromosome control a single characteristic. The presence of freckles in the human skin, for example, is believed to be due to the influence of a single pair of genes.

Each cell of the body contains the specific number of paired chromosomes characteristic of the organism. Because each type of gene is present on both chromosomes of a chromosome pair, *each type of gene is therefore present in duplicate*. The fusion of a sperm cell from the male with an egg cell from the female, as occurs in fertilization, should therefore result in offspring having a *quadruplicate number* (4) of each type of gene. Mating of these individuals would then produce progeny having an *octuplicate number* (8) of each type of gene, and so on. This, however, is normally prevented by a special process. When ordinary body cells prepare to divide to form more tissue, each pair of chromosomes duplicates itself so that there are four partner chromosomes of each kind instead of only two. When the cell divides, two of the four partners, or one pair, go into each new cell. This process, known as *MITOSIS,* insures that each new body cell contains the proper number of chromosomes. Reproductive cells (sperm cell and egg cells), however, undergo a special kind of division known as *MEIOSIS*. In meiosis, the chromosome pairs do *not* duplicate themselves, and thus when the reproductive cells reach the final dividing stage only one chromosome, or one-half of the pair, goes into each new reproductive cell. Each reproductive cell, therefore, has only half the normal number of chromosomes. These are referred to as *HAPLOID* cells, in contrast to *DIPLOID* cells, which have the full number of chromosomes.

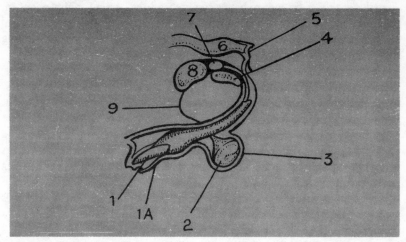

The reproductive system of a male: 1a, sheath; 1, penis; 2, testicle; 3, scrotum; 4, pelvic bone; 5, anus; 6, rectum; 7, prostate; 8, bladder; 9, vas deferens.

When the haploid sperm cell fuses with the haploid egg cell in fertilization, the resulting offspring has the normal diploid number of chromosomes.

If both partner genes, or alleles, affect the trait in an identical manner, the genes are said to be *HOMOZYGOUS,* but if one affects the character in a manner different from the other gene, or allele, the genes are said to be *HETEROZYGOUS.* For example, in the pair of genes affecting eye color in humans, if each gene of the pair produces blue eyes, the genes (and also the person carrying the genes) are said to be homozygous for blue eyes. If, however, one gene of the pair produces blue eyes, while the other gene, or allele, produces brown eyes, they are said to be heterozygous. The presence of heterozygous genes raises the question, *"Will the offspring have blue eyes or brown eyes?"* which in turn introduces another genetic principle: *DOMINANCE* and *RECESSIVENESS.*

If one gene of a pair can block the action of its partner, or allele, while still producing its own affect, that gene is said to be *dominant* over its allele. Its allele, on the other hand, is said to be recessive. In the case of heterozygous genes for eye color, the brown eye gene is dominant over the recessive blue eye gene, and the offspring therefore will have brown eyes. Much less common is the occurrence of gene pairs in which neither gene is completely dominant over the other. This, known as *INCOMPLETE* or *PARTIAL DOMINANCE,* results in a blending of the opposing influences. In cattle, if a homozygous (pure) red bull is mated with a homozygous (pure) white cow, the calf will be roan, a blending of red and white hairs in its coat, rather than either all red or all white.

During meiosis, or division of the reproductive (sperm and egg) cells, each pair of chromosomes splits, and one-half of each pair goes into one of the two new cells. Thus, in the case of eye color genes, one new reproductive cell will get the chromosome carrying the blue eye gene, while the other new reproductive cell will get the chromosome carrying the brown eye gene, and so on for each pair of chromosomes. If an organism has only two pairs of chromosomes — called pair A, made up of chromosomes A_1 and A_2, and pair B, made up of chromosomes B_1 and B_2 — each new reproductive cell will get one chromosome from each pair, and four different combinations are possible: A_1 and B_1; A_1 and B_2; A_2 and B_1, or A_2 and B_2. If the blue eye gene is on A_1, the brown eye gene on A_2, the gene for curly hair on B_1 and the gene for straight hair on B_2, each of the above combinations will exert a different genetic effect on the offspring. This different grouping of chromosomes in the new reproductive cell as a result of meiotic cell division is known as *INDEPENDENT ASSORTMENT* and is one reason why variation occurs in the offspring. In the dog, with 39 pairs of chromosomes, the possibilities of variation through independent assortment are tremendous.

But variation does not end here. For example, if two dominant genes, such as the genes for brown eyes and dark hair, were on the same chromosome, all brown-eyed people would have dark hair. Yet in instances where such joined or *LINKED* genes do occur, the two characteristics do not always appear together in the same offspring. This is due to a process known as *CROSS-OVER* or *RECOMBINATION*. Recombination is the mutual exchange of corresponding blocks of genes between the two chromosomes in a pair. That is, during cell division, the two chromosomes may exchange their tip sections or other corresponding segments. If the segments exchanged contain the eye color genes, the brown eye gene will be transferred from the chromosome carrying the dark hair gene to the chromosome carrying the light hair gene, and then brown eyes will occur with light hair, provided that the individual is homozygous for the recessive light hair gene.

Another important source of variation is *MUTATION*. In mutation, a gene becomes altered, such as by exposure to irradiation, and exerts a different effect than it did before. Most mutations are harmful to the organism, and some may result in death. Offspring carrying mutated genes and showing the effects of these mutations are known as *MUTANTS* or *SPORTS*. Mutation also means that instead of only two alleles for eye color, such as brown and blue, there may now be three or more (gray, black, etc.) creating a much larger source for possible variation in the offspring.

Further complications in the transmission and appearance of genetic traits are the phenomena known as *EPISTASIS* and *PLEIOTROPY*. Epistasis refers to a gene exerting influence on genes other than its own allele.

In all-white red-eyed (albino) guinea pigs, for example, the gene controlling intensity of color is epistatic to any other color gene and prevents that gene from producing its effect. Thus, even if a gene for red spots were present in the cells of the guinea pig, the color intensity gene would prevent the red spots from appearing in the guinea pig's white coat. *Pleiotropy* refers to the fact that a single gene may control a number of characteristics. In the fruit fly, for example, the gene that controls eye color may also affect the structure of certain body parts and even the lifespan of the insect.

One special pair of chromosomes is known as the sex chromosomes. In man, dog, and other mammals, these chromosomes are of two types, designated as X and Y. Under normal conditions, a mammal carrying two X-type sex chromosomes is a female, whereas a mammal carrying one X-type and one Y-type is a male. Females, therefore, have only X chromosomes and can only contribute X chromosomes to the offspring, but the male may contribute either an X or a Y.

If the male's sperm carrying an X chromosome fertilizes the female's egg cell (X), the offspring (XX) will be female; if a sperm carrying a Y chromosome fertilizes the egg (X), the offspring (XY) will be male. It is the male, therefore, that determines the sex of the offspring in mammals.

Traits controlled by genes present on the sex chromosome, and which appear in only one sex, are said to be *SEX LINKED*. If, for example, a rare recessive gene occurs on the X chromosome, it cannot exert its effect in the female because the dominant allele on the other X chromosome will counteract it. In the male, however, there is no second X chromosome, and if the Y chromosome cannot offer any countereffect, the recessive character will appear. There are also *SEX-LIMITED* characteristics: these appear primarily or solely in one sex, but the genes for these traits are not carried on the sex chromosomes. Sex-limited traits appear when genes on other chromosomes exert their effect in the proper hormonal (male or female) environment. Sex-linked and sex-limited transmission is how a trait may skip a generation, by being passed from grandfather to grandson through a mother in which the trait, though present, does not show.

In dealing with the simplest form of heredity — one gene effecting one character — there is an expected ratio of the offspring displaying the character to those who do not display it, depending upon the genetic makeup of the parents. If a parent is homozygous for a character, such as blue eyes, it makes no difference which half of the chromosome pair enters the new reproductive cell, because each chromosome carries the gene for blue eyes. If a parent is heterozygous, however, one reproductive cell will receive the brown eye gene while the other will receive the blue eye gene. If both parents are homozygous for blue eyes, all the offspring will receive two blue eye genes, and all will have blue eyes. If a parent is homozygous for blue eyes, and the other parent is homozygous for brown eyes, all the offspring will be heterozygous, receiving one brown eye gene and one blue eye gene, and because brown is dominant, all will have brown eyes. If both parents are heterozygous, both the blue eye gene and the brown eye gene from one parent have an equal likelihood of ending up with either the blue eye or the brown eye gene from the other parent. This results in a ratio of two heterozygous offspring to the one homozygous for brown eyes and one homozygous for blue eyes, giving a total genetic, or genotypic, ratio of 2:1:1 or, as it is more commonly arranged, 1:2:1. As the two heterozygous as well as the homozygous brown eye offspring will have brown eyes, the ratio of brown eyes to blue eyes (or phenotypic ratio) will be 3:1.

If one parent is heterozygous and the other parent is homozygous for the recessive gene for blue eyes, half of the offspring will be homozygous for blue eyes and will have blue eyes, but the other half of the offspring will be heterozygous and have brown eyes. (Here both the genotypic and phenotypic ratio is 1:1.)

If the homozygous parent, however, has the dominant gene (brown eyes), half of the offspring will be heterozygous and half will be homozygous, as before, but all will have brown eyes. By repeated determinations of these ratios in the offspring, geneticists are able to analyze the genetic makeup of the parents.

Before leaving heredity, it might be well to explain the difference between inbreeding, outcrossing, line breeding, and similar terms. Basically, there are only inbreeding and outbreeding. Inbreeding, however, according to its intensity, is usually divided into inbreeding proper and line breeding. Inbreeding proper is considered to be the mating of very closely related individuals, generally within the immediate family, but this is sometimes extended to include matings to first cousins and grandparents. Line breeding is the mating of more distantly related animals, that is, animals, not immediately related to each other but having a common ancestor, such as the same grandsire or great-grandsire. Outbreeding is divided into outcrossing, which is the mating of dogs from different families within the same breed, and cross-breeding, which is mating purebred dogs from different breeds.

From the foregoing discussion of genetics, it should be realized that the theory of telegony, which states that the sire of one litter can influence future litters sired by other studs, is simply not true; it is possible, however, if several males mate with a female during a single estrus cycle, that the various puppies in the litter may have different sires (but not two sires for any one puppy). It should also be realized that blood does not really enter into the transmission of inheritance, although people commonly speak of "bloodlines," "pure-blooded," etc.

7. Care of the Mother and Family

PRENATAL CARE OF THE FEMALE

You can expect the puppies nine weeks from the day of breeding, although 58 days is as common as 63. During this time the female should receive normal care and exercise. If she is overweight, don't increase her food at first; excess weight at whelping time is not good. If she is on the thin side, build her up, giving her a morning meal of cereal and egg yolk. Consult your veterinarian as to increasing her vitamins and mineral supplement. During the last weeks the puppies grow enormously, and the mother will have little room for food and less appetite. Divide her meals into smaller portions and feed her more ofen. If she loses her appetite, tempt her with meat, liver, chicken, etc.

As she grows heavier, eliminate violent exercise and jumping. Do not eliminate exercise entirely, as walking is beneficial to the female in whelp, and mild exercise will maintain her muscle tone in preparation for the birth. Weigh your female after breeding and keep a record of her weight each week thereafter. Groom your bitch daily — some females have a slight discharge during gestation, more prevalent during the last two weeks, so wash the vulva with warm water daily. Usually, by the end of the fifth week you can notice a broadening across her loins, and her breasts become firmer. By the end of the sixth week your veterinarian can tell you whether or not she is pregnant.

PREPARATION OF WHELPING QUARTERS

Prepare a whelping box at least a week before the puppies are to arrive and allow the mother-to-be to sleep there overnight or to spend some time in it during the day to become accustomed to it. She is then less likely to try to have her litter under the front porch or in the middle of your bed.

The box should have a wooden floor. Sides should be high enough to keep the puppies in but low enough to allow the mother to get out after she has fed them. Layers of newspapers spread over the whole area will make excellent bedding and will be absorbent enough to keep the surface warm and dry. They should be removed when wet or soiled and replaced with another thick layer. An old quilt or blanket is more comfortable for the mother and makes better footing for the nursing puppies, at least during the first week, than slippery newspaper. The quilt should be secured firmly.

SUPPLIES TO HAVE ON HAND

As soon as you have the whelping box prepared, set up the nursery by collecting the various supplies you will need when the puppies arrive. You should have the following items on hand: a box lined with towels for the puppies, a heating pad or hot water bottle to keep the puppy box warm, a pile of clean terrycloth towels or washcloths to remove membranes and to dry puppies, a stack of folded newspapers, a roll of paper towels, vaseline, rubber gloves, soap, iodine, muzzle, cotton balls, a small pair of blunt scissors to cut umbilical cords (stick them into an open bottle of alcohol so they keep freshly sterilized), a rectal thermometer, white thread, a flashlight in case the electricity goes off, a waste container, and a scale for weighing each puppy at birth.

It is necessary that the whelping room be warm and free from drafts, because puppies are delivered wet from the mother. Keep a little notebook and pencil handy so you can record the duration of the first labor and the time between the arrival of each puppy. If there is trouble in whelping, this is the information that the veterinarian will want. Keep his telephone number handy in case you have to call him in an emergency, and warn him to be prepared for an emergency, should you need him.

WHELPING

Be prepared for the actual whelping several days in advance. Usually the female will tear up papers, try to dig nests, refuse food, and generally act restless and nervous. These may be false alarms; the real test is her temperature, which will drop to below 100° about twelve hours before whelping. Take her temperature rectally at a set time each day, starting about a week before she is due to whelp. After her temperature goes down, keep her constantly with you or put her in the whelping box and stay in the room with her. She will seem anxious and look to you for reassurance. Be prepared to remove the membranes covering the puppy's head if the mother fails to do this, for the puppy could smother otherwise.

The mother should start licking the puppy as soon as it is out of the sac, thus drying and stimulating it, but if she does not perform this task you can do it with a soft rough towel, instead. The afterbirth should follow the birth of each puppy, attached to the puppy by the umbilical cord. Watch to make sure that each is expelled, for retaining this material can cause infection. The mother probably will eat the afterbirth after biting the cord. One or two will not hurt her; they stimulate milk supply as well as labor for remaining puppies. Too many, however, can make her lose her appetite for the food she needs to feed her puppies and regain her strength, so remove the rest of them along with the soiled newspapers, and keep the box dry and clean to relieve her anxiety.

If a puppy does not start breathing, wrap him in a towel, hold him upside down with his head toward the ground, and shake him vigorously. If he still does not breathe, rub his ribs briskly; if this also fails, administer artificial respiration by compressing the ribs about twenty times per minute.

If the mother does not bite the cord, or bites it too close to the body, you should take over the job to prevent an umbilical hernia. Cut the cord a short distance from the body with your blunt scissors. Put a drop of iodine on the end of the cord; it will dry up and fall off in a few days.

The puppies should follow each other at regular intervals, but deliveries can be as short as five minutes or as long as two hours apart. A puppy may be presented backwards; if the mother does not seem to be in trouble, do not interfere. But if enough of the puppy is outside the birth canal, use a rough towel and help her by pulling gently on the puppy. Pull only when she pushes. A rear-first, or breech, birth can cause a puppy to strangle on its own umbilical cord, so don't let the mother struggle too long. Breech birth is quite common.

When you think all the puppies have been whelped, have your veterinarian examine the mother to determine if all the afterbirths have been expelled. He will probably give her an injection to be certain that the uterus is clean, a shot of calcium for prevention of eclampsia, and possibly an injection of penicillin to prevent infection.

RAISING THE PUPPIES

Hold each puppy to a breast as soon as you have dried him. This will be an opportunity to have a good meal without competition. Then place him in the small box that you have prepared so he will be out of his mother's way while she is whelping. Keep a record of birth weights and take weekly readings thereafter so that you will have an accurate account of the puppies' growth. After the puppies have arrived, take the mother outside for a walk and a drink, and then leave her to take care of them. Offer her a dish of vanilla ice cream or milk with corn syrup in it. She usually will eat lying down while the puppies are nursing and will appreciate the coolness of the ice cream during warm weather or in a hot room. She will not want to stay away from her puppies more than a minute or two the first few weeks. Be sure to keep water available at all times, and feed her milk or broth frequently, as she needs liquids to produce milk. To encourage her to eat, offer her the foods she likes best, until she "asks" to be fed without your tempting her. She will soon develop a ravenous appetite and should be fed whenever she is hungry.

Be sure that all the puppies are getting enough to eat. Cut their claws with special dog "nail" clippers, as they grow rapidly and scratch the mother as the puppies nurse. Normally the puppies should be completely weaned by six weeks, although you may start to give them supplementary feedings at three weeks. They will find it easier to lap semi-solid food.

As the puppies grow up, the mother will go into the box only to nurse them, first sitting up and then standing. To dry up her milk supply completely, keep her away from her puppies for longer periods. After a few days of part-time nursing she will be able to stay away for much longer periods of time, and then completely. The little milk left will be resorbed.

When the puppies are five weeks old, consult your veterinarian about temporary shots to protect them against distemper and hepatitis; it is quite possible for dangerous infectious germs to reach them even though you keep their living quarters sanitary. You can expect the puppies to need at least one worming before they are ready to go to their new homes, so take a stool sample to your veterinarian before they are three weeks old. If one puppy has worms, all should be wormed. Follow your veterinarian's advice.

The puppies may be put outside, unless it is too cold, as soon as their eyes are open (about ten days), and they will benefit from the sunlight. A rubber mat or newspapers underneath their box will protect them from cold or dampness.

HOW TO TAKE CARE OF A LARGE LITTER

The size of a litter varies greatly. If your bitch has a large litter she may have trouble feeding all of the puppies. You can help her by preparing an extra puppy box. Leave half the litter with the mother and the other half in a warm place, changing their places at two-hour intervals at first. Later you may change them less frequently, leaving them all together except during the day. Try supplementary feeding, too, as soon as their eyes are open.

CAESAREAN SECTION

If your female goes into hard labor and is not able to give birth within two hours, you will know that there is something wrong. Call your veterinarian for advice. Some females must have Caesarean sections (taking puppies from the mother by surgery), but don't be alarmed if your dog has to undergo this. The operation is relatively safe. She can be taken to the veterinarian, operated on, and then be back in her whelping box at home within three hours, with all puppies nursing normally a short time later.

8. Health

WATCHING YOUR PUPPY'S HEALTH

First, don't be frightened by the number of diseases a dog can contract. The majority of dogs never get any of them. Don't become a dog-hypochondriac. All dogs have days when they feel lazy and want to lie around doing nothing. For the few diseases that you might be concerned about, remember that your veterinarian is your dog's best friend. When you first get your puppy, select a veterinarian who you feel is qualified to treat dogs. He will get to know your dog and will be glad to have you consult him for advice. A dog needs little medical care, but that little is essential to his good health and well-being. He needs:

1. Proper diet at regular hours
2. Clean, roomy housing
3. Daily exercise
4. Companionship and love
5. Frequent grooming
6. Regular check-ups by your veterinarian

THE USEFUL THERMOMETER

Almost every serious ailment shows itself by an increase in the dog's body temperature. If your dog acts lifeless, looks dull-eyed, and gives the impression of illness, check his temperature by using a rectal thermometer. Hold the dog and insert the thermometer, which should be lubricated with vaseline, and take a reading. The average normal temperature is 101.5° F. Excitement may raise this value slightly, but any rise of more than a few points is a cause for alarm. Consult your veterinarian.

FIRST AID

In general, a dog will heal his wounds by licking them. If he swallows anything harmful, chances are that he will throw it up. But it will probably make you feel better to help him if he is hurt, so treat his wounds as you would your own. Wash out the dirt and apply an antiseptic. If you are afraid that your dog has swallowed poison and you can't get to the veterinarian fast enough, try to induce vomiting by giving him a strong solution of salt water or mustard and water. Amateur diagnosis is dangerous, because the symptoms of so many dog diseases are alike. Too many people wait too long to take their dog to the doctor.

IMPORTANCE OF INOCULATIONS

With the proper series of inoculations, your dog will be almost completely protected against disease. However, it occasionally happens that the shot does not take, and sometimes a different form of the virus appears against which your dog may not be protected.

DISTEMPER

Probably the most virulent of all dog diseases is distemper. Young dogs are most susceptible to it, although it may affect dogs of all ages. The dog will lose his appetite, seem depressed, chilled, and run a fever. Often he will have a watery discharge from his eyes and nose. Unless treated promptly, the disease goes into advanced stages with infections of the lungs, intestines, and nervous system, and dogs that recover may be left with some impairment such as paralysis, convulsions, a twitch, or some other defect, usually spastic in nature. The best protection against this is very early inoculation with a series of permanent shots and a booster shot each year thereafter.

HEPATITIS

Veterinarians report an increase in the spread of this viral disease in recent years, usually with younger dogs as the victims. The initial symptoms — drowsiness, vomiting, great thirst, loss of appetite, and a high temperature — closely resemble those of distemper. These symptoms are often accompanied by swellings of the head, neck, and abdomen. The disease strikes quickly; death may occur in just a few hours. Protection is afforded by injection with a vaccine recently developed.

LEPTOSPIROSIS

This disease is caused by bacteria that live in stagnant or slow-moving water. It is carried by rats and dogs; infection is begun by the dog's licking substances contaminated by the urine or feces of infected animals. The symptoms are diarrhea and a yellowish-brown discoloration of the jaws, tongue, and teeth, caused by an inflammation of the kidneys. This disease can be cured if caught in time, but it is best to ward it off with a vaccine which your veterinarian can administer along with the distemper shots.

RABIES

This is an acute disease of the dog's central nervous system. It is spread by infectious saliva transmitted by the bite of an infected animal. Rabies is generally manifested in one of two classes of symptoms. The first is "furious rabies," in which the dog shows a period of melancholy or depression, then irritation, and finally paralysis. The first period lasts from a few hours to several days. During this time the dog is cross and will change his position often. He loses his appetite for food and begins to lick, bite, and swallow foreign objects. During the irritative phase the dog is spasmodically wild and has impulses to run away. He acts in a fearless manner and runs and bites at everything in sight. If he is caged or confined he will fight at the bars, often breaking teeth or fracturing his jaw. His bark becomes a peculiar howl. In the final, or paralytic, stage, the animal's lower jaw becomes paralyzed and hangs down; he walks with a stagger and saliva drips from his mouth. Within four to eight days after the onset of paralysis, the dog dies.

The second class of symptoms is referred to as "dumb rabies" and is characterized by the dog's walking in a bearlike manner, head down. The lower jaw is paralyzed and the dog is unable to bite. Outwardly it may seem as though he had a bone caught in his throat.

Even if your pet should be bitten by a rabid dog or other animal, he probably can be saved if you get him to the veterinarian in time for a series of injections. However, after the symptoms have appeared no cure is possible. But remember that an annual rabies inoculation is almost certain protection against rabies. If you suspect your dog of rabies, notify your local Health Department. A rabid dog is a danger to all who come near him.

COUGHS, COLDS, BRONCHITIS, PNEUMONIA

Respiratory diseases may affect the dog because he is forced to live under man-made conditions rather than in his natural environment. Being subjected to cold or a draft after a bath, sleeping near an air conditioner or in the path of a fan or near a radiator can cause respiratory ailments. The symptoms are similar to those in humans. The germs of these diseases, however, are different and do not affect both dogs and humans, so they cannot be infected by each other. Treatment is much the same as for a child with the same type of illness. Keep the dog warm, quiet, and well fed. Your veterinarian has antibiotics and other remedies to help the dog recover.

INTERNAL PARASITES

There are four common internal parasites that may infect your dog. These are roundworms, hookworms, whipworms, and tapeworms. The first three can be diagnosed by laboratory examination; the presence of tapeworms is determined by seeing segments in the stool or attached to the hair around the tail. Do not under any circumstances attempt to worm your dog without the advice of your veterinarian. After first determining what type of worm or worms are present, he will advise you of the best method of treatment.

EXTERNAL PARASITES

The dog that is groomed regularly and provided with clean sleeping quarters should not be troubled by fleas, ticks, or lice. If the dog should become infested with any of these parasites, he should be treated with a medicated dip bath or the new oral medications that are presently available.

SKIN AILMENTS

Any persistent scratching may indicate an irritation. Whenever you groom your dog, look for the reddish spots that may indicate eczema, mange, or fungal infection. Rather than treating your dog yourself, take him to the

NYLABONE® is a necessity that is available at your local petshop (not in supermarkets). The puppy or grown dog chews the hambone flavored nylon into a frilly dog toothbrush, massaging his gums and cleaning his teeth as he plays. Veterinarians highly recommend this product . , . but beware of cheap imitations which might splinter or break.

veterinarian, as some of the conditions may be difficult to eradicate and can cause permanent damage to his coat.

EYES, EARS, TEETH, AND CLAWS

If you notice foreign matter collecting in the corners of your dog's eyes, wipe it out with a piece of cotton or tissue. If there is a discharge, check with your veterinarian.

Examine your dog's ears daily. Remove all visible wax, using a piece of cotton dipped in a boric acid solution or a solution of equal parts of water and hydrogen peroxide. Be gentle and don't probe into the ear, but just clean the parts you can see.

Don't give your dog bones to chew: they can choke him or puncture his intestines. Today veterinarians and dog experts recommend Nylabone, a synthetic bone manufactured by a secret process, that can't splinter or break even when pounded by a hammer. Nylabone will keep puppies from chewing furniture, aid in relieving the aching gums of a teething pup, and act as a toothbrush for the older dog, preventing the accumulation of tartar. Check your dog's mouth regularly and, as he gets older, have your veterinarian clean his teeth twice a year.

To clip your dog's claws, use specially designed clippers that are available at your petshop. Never take off too much of the claw, as you might

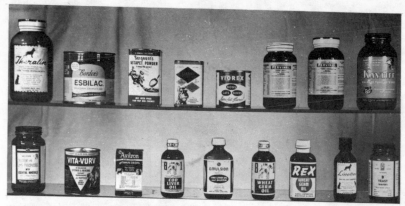

Active dogs and breeding bitches need food supplements. Visit your petshop for fresh vitamins and minerals to be added to your dog's diet.

cut the quick, which is sensitive and will bleed. Be particularly careful when you cut claws in which the quick is not visible. If you have any doubts about being able to cut your dog's claws, have your veterinarian or petshop do it periodically.

CARE OF THE AGED DOG

With the increased knowledge and care available, there is no reason why your dog should not live to a good old age. As the years go by he may need a little additional care. Remember that an excessively fat dog is not healthy, particularly as he grows older, so limit the older dog's food accordingly. He needs exercise as much as ever, although his heart cannot bear the strain of sudden and violent exertion. Failing eyesight or hearing means lessened awareness of dangers, so you must protect him more than ever.

Should you decide at this time to get a puppy, to avoid being without a dog when your old friend is no longer with you, be very careful how you introduce the puppy. He naturally will be playful and will expect the older dog to respond to his advances. Sometimes the old dog will get a new lease on life from a new puppy, but he may be consumed with jealousy. Do not give the newcomer the attention that formerly was exclusively the older dog's. Feed them apart, and show your old friend that you still love him the most; the puppy, not being accustomed to individual attention, will not mind sharing your love.

9. Showing

There is no greater pleasure for the owner than showing a beautiful dog perfectly groomed and trained for the show ring. Whether he wins or not, it is gratifying to show a dog in superb condition, one that is a credit to your training and care. A great deal of preparation, both for you and your dog, is needed before the day that you do any serious winning. Showing is not so easy as it looks, even if you have a magnificent dog. He must be presented to the judge so that all of his good points are shown to advantage. This requires practice in gaiting, daily grooming from puppyhood, and the proper diet to make him sound in body.

When you buy your puppy you probably will think he is the best in the country and possibly in the world, but before you enter the highly competitive world of dog shows, get some unbiased expert opinion. As your dog matures, compare him with the standard of his breed. Visit a few dog shows as a spectator and make mental notes of what is required of the handlers and dogs. Watch how the experienced handlers manage their dogs to bring out their best points.

TYPES OF DOG SHOWS

There are various types of dog shows. The American Kennel Club sanctioned matches are shows at which purebred dogs may compete, but not for championship points. These are excellent for you to enter to accustom you and your dog to showing. If your dog places in a few match shows, then you might seriously consider entering the big-time shows. An American Kennel Club all-breed show is one at which purebred dogs compete for championship points. An American Kennel Club specialty show is for one breed only. It may be held in conjunction with an all-breed show (by designating the classes at that show as its specialty show) or it may be held entirely apart. Obedience trials are different in that in them the dog is judged according to his obedience and ability to perform, not by his conformation to the breed standard.

There are two types of championship conformation shows: *benched* and *unbenched*. At a benched show your dog must be on his appointed bench during the advertised hours of the show's duration. He may be removed from the bench only to be taken to the exercise pen or to be groomed (an hour before showing) in an area designated for handlers to set up their crates and grooming tables. At an unbenched show your car may serve as a bench for your dog.

To become a champion your dog must win fifteen points in competition with other dogs; a portion of the fifteen points must be awarded as major point wins (three to five points) under different judges.

HOW TO ENTER

If your dog is purebred and registered with the AKC — or eligible for registration — you may enter him in the appropriate show class for which his age, sex, and previous show record qualify him. You will find coming shows listed in the different dog magazines or at your petshop. Write to the secretary of the show, asking for the premium list. When you receive the entry form, fill it in carefully and send it back with the required entry fee. Then, before the show, you should receive your exhibitor's pass, which will admit you and your dog to the show. Here are the five official show classes:

PUPPY CLASS: Open to dogs at least six months and not more than twelve months of age. Limited to dogs whelped in the United States and Canada.

NOVICE CLASS: Open to dogs six months of age or older that have never won a first prize in any class other than the puppy class, and less than three first prizes in the novice class itself. Limited to dogs whelped in the United States or Canada.

BRED BY EXHIBITOR CLASS: Open to all dogs, except champions, six months of age or over which are exhibited by the same person, or his immediate family, or kennel that was the recognized breeder on the records of the American Kennel Club.

AMERICAN-BRED CLASS: Open to dogs that are not champions, six months of age or over, whelped in the United States after a mating which took place in the United States.

OPEN CLASS: Open to dogs six months of age or over, with no exceptions.

In addition there are local classes, the Specials Only class, and brace and team entries.

For full information on dog shows, read the book *HOW TO SHOW YOUR OWN DOG,* by Virginia Tuck Nichols. (T.F.H.)

ADVANCED PREPARATION

Before you go to a show your dog should be trained to gait at a trot beside you, with head up and in a straight line. In the ring you will have to gait your dog around the edge with other dogs and then individually up and down the center runner. In addition the dog must stand for examination by the judge, who will look at him closely and feel his head and body structure. He should be taught to stand squarely, hind feet slightly back, head up on the alert. Showing requires practice training sessions in advance. Get a friend to act as judge and set the dog up and "show" him a few minutes every day.

Sometime before the show, give your dog a bath so he will look his best. Get together all the things you will need to take to the show. You will want to take a water dish and a bottle of water for your dog (so he won't be affected by a change in drinking water). Take your show lead, bench chain (if it is a benched show), combs and brush, and the identification ticket sent by the show superintendent, noting the time you must be there and the place where the show will be held, as well as the time of judging.

THE DAY OF THE SHOW

Don't feed your dog the morning of the show, or give him at most a light meal. He will be more comfortable in the car on the way, and will show more enthusiastically. When you arrive at the show grounds, find out where he is to be benched and settle him there. Your bench or stall number is on your identification ticket, and the breed name will be on placards fastened to the ends of the row of benches. Once you have your dog securely fastened to his stall by a bench chain (use a bench crate instead of a chain if you prefer), locate the ring where your dog will be judged (the number and time of showing will be on the program of judging which came with your ticket). After this you may want to take your dog to the exercise ring to relieve himself, and give him a small drink of water. Your dog will have been groomed before the show, but give him a final brushing just before going into the show ring. When your breed judging is called, it is your responsibility to be at the ringside ready to go in. The steward will give you an armband which has on it the number of your dog.

Then, as you step into the ring, try to keep your knees from knocking! Concentrate on your dog and before you realize it you'll be out again, perhaps back with the winners of each class for more judging and finally, with luck, it will be over and you'll have a ribbon and trophy — and, of course, the most wonderful dog in the world.

BIBLIOGRAPHY

PS-606 DOLLARS IN DOGS, by Leon F. Whitney, D.V.M. The 26 chapters of this beautifully useful book tell you—frankly and clearly—how you can make money in the dog field. Every avenue to profit through dogs is explored thoroughly by Dr. Whitney, famous veterinarian and breeder. There are no punches pulled in the discussions of money-making opportunities available to everyone who wants to profit through his connection with canines. A real career-builder, 254 pages of solid and practical information, illustrated.
ISBN #0-87666-290-4
8½ x 5½ 255 pages 60 black & white photos

PS-684 DOG HOROSCOPE—YOUR DOG NEEDS A BIRTH-
DAY. Probably the most clever and entertaining dog book ever
published. Illustrated in color, readers are in for 64 pages of informative amusement, and you don't have to be an astrology fan
to enjoy it.
ISBN #0-87666-317-X
8 x 5½ 64 pages 14 line illustrations

PS-607 HOW TO SHOW YOUR OWN DOG, by Virginia Tuck
Nichols, paves the highroad to success in the fascinating and
steadily growing avocation of exhibiting dogs. All of the intrica-
cies of the show ring are explained in detail, coupled with won-
derfully explicit treatments of the basics of dog shows; terms and
definitions, how a champion is made, getting ready for the show,
AKC rules and regulations, etc. Plus a bonus chapter on the
tricks of the trade. In all, 254 well-illustrated pages that make
winning in the dog show ring easier and a lot more fun.
ISBN #0-87666-390-0
8 ½ x 5½ 254 pages 136 black & white photos 10 line illustrations

H-925 DOG BREEDERS' HANDBOOK, by Ernest H. Hart. Here
is the most complete and authoritative book on breeding ever
written. In layman's language it clarifies all areas of this very
necessary but often misunderstood subject. Beautifully presented and authored by a professional writer and recognized dog au-
thority, the written word is augmented by profuse and pertinent
illustrations.
ISBN #0-87666-286-6
85 black & white photos 12 line illustrations

PS-644 HOW TO TRAIN YOUR DOG, by Ernest H. Hart. Any dog
is a better dog when well-trained. With the help of this book, any
owner can do a first class job of training his dog. Fully and completely illustrated, the author takes you step by advancing step
through the various areas of training. Many vital new concepts of
training are advanced and discussed in this invaluable book. Col-
or and black and white illustrations.
ISBN #0-87666-284-X
8½ x 5½ 107 pages 95 black & white photos 31 color photos

H-934 DOG OWNER'S ENCYCLOPEDIA OF VETERINARY
MEDICINE, by Dr. Allan Hart. Here is a book that will become,
next to his pet itself, the truest friend a dog-owner has. Page after
page and chapter after chapter of valuable, pertinent information that allows an owner to make sure that his pet is given the
best of care at all times. Easy to read yet brilliantly informative,
this big book is a must.
ISBN #0-87666-287-4
8 x 5½ 186 pages 61 black & white photos 25 line illustrations

Amazing Mammals

by Lisa M. Herrington

Content Consultant
Dr. Lucy Spelman
Zoological Medicine Specialist

Reading Consultant
Jeanne M. Clidas, Ph.D.
Reading Specialist

Children's Press®
An Imprint of Scholastic Inc.

Library of Congress Cataloging-in-Publication Data
Herrington, Lisa M., author.
Amazing mammals/by Lisa M. Herrington.
    pages cm. — (Rookie read about science. Strange animals)
Summary: "Introduces the reader to amazing animals." —Provided by publisher.
Includes index.
ISBN 978-0-531-22600-1 (library binding) — ISBN 978-0-531-22746-6 (pbk.)
    1. Mammals—Miscellanea—Juvenile literature. 2. Children's questions and answers.
I. Title.
QL706.2.H47 2016
    599.02—dc23   2015021143

Produced by Spooky Cheetah Press
Design by Keith Plechaty

© 2016 by Scholastic Inc.

All rights reserved. Published in 2016 by Children's Press, an imprint of Scholastic Inc.

Printed in China 62

SCHOLASTIC, CHILDREN'S PRESS, ROOKIE READ-ABOUT®, and associated logos
are trademarks and/or registered trademarks of Scholastic Inc.

1 2 3 4 5 6 7 8 9 10 R 25 24 23 22 21 20 19 18 17 16

Photographs ©: cover: Steve Bloom Images/Superstock, Inc.; 3 top left: Patryk
Kosmider/Shutterstock, Inc.; 3 top right: Neirfy/Shutterstock, Inc.; 3 bottom: Anan
Kaewkhammul/Shutterstock, Inc.; 4: age fotostock/Superstock, Inc.; 7: NHPA/
Superstock, Inc.; 8: Suzi Eszterhas/Minden Pictures; 11: Tony Camacho/Science
Source; 12: Minden Pictures/Superstock, Inc.; 15: Patrick Shyu/National Geographic
Creative; 16 left: J & C Sohns/Superstock, Inc.; 16 center, 16 right: Tier und
Naturfotografie/Superstock, Inc.; 19: Ken Catania/Visuals Unlimited; 20 top: Roland
Seitre/Minden Pictures; 20 bottom: Kristian Bell/Shutterstock, Inc.; 23 main: John
Warden/Superstock, Inc.; 23 inset: louise murray/Alamy Images; 24: Brian J. Skerry/
National Geographic Creative; 26: Efired/Shutterstock, Inc.; 27: Mint Images/
Superstock, Inc.; 28 background, 29 background: Zack Frank/Shutterstock, Inc.; 28
top: Animals Animals/Superstock, Inc.; 28 bottom: age fotostock/Superstock, Inc.;
29 top: NaturePL/Superstock, Inc.; 29 center: Denis Palanque/Biosphoto; 29 bottom
left: Biosphoto/Superstock, Inc.; 29 bottom right: Amy Harris/Dreamstime; 30:
imageBROKER/Superstock, Inc.; 31 top: Tony Camacho/Science Source; 31 center
top: Biosphoto/Superstock, Inc.; 31 center bottom: Minden Pictures/Superstock, Inc.;
31 bottom: Patrick Shyu/National Geographic Creative.